TWENTY + CHANGE

EMERGING CANADIAN DESIGN PRACTICES

03

edited by
Heather Dubbeldam
Lola Sheppard

Riverside Architectural Press

Twenty + Change 03

Editors: Heather Dubbeldam, Lola Sheppard
Design & Production: Fionn Byrne, Heather Dubbeldam, Lola Sheppard
Copy-editor: Doris Cowan

Printing by Astley Gilbert Limited, Toronto
This book was set in Slate Std and Univers LT Std.

Special thanks to the following individuals:

Our curatorial committee: Marc Boutin, Renée Daoust, Miyoko Ohtake,
Larry Wayne Richards, Talbot Sweetapple

Our volunteers and advisors: Donna Bridgeman, Ian Chodikoff, Oliver Dang,
Jacob JeBailey, Leslie Jen, Bindya Lad, Thomas Nemeskeri, Miriam Ng

Those who helped make this book possible: Fionn Byrne, Doris Cowan,
Antonio Gomez-Palacio, Kevin McIntosh, Mason White, Wayne Wilbur

Special thanks to our sponsors:
Lead Sponsor:

Additional sponsors:
Canada Council for the Arts, Astley Gilbert Limited, Ciot, Forbo Flooring
Systems, Blackwell Bowick Partnership Limited, Engineered Assemblies,
Stone Tile International Inc., Royal Architectural Institute of Canada

Canada Council   Conseil des Arts
for the Arts   du Canada

Published with the generous assistance of the Canada Council for the Arts.

ISBN:978-1-926724-12-6

Contents

Preface

The organizers of this second iteration of Twenty + Change as a national initiative can take pleasure in knowing that it provides Canada with a much-needed stage for discourse on contemporary architecture. The celebration of emergent architectural practices within Canada through the selection of design excellence in their commissioned creative work is no simple task, and thereby speaks to the effort, skill and tenacity of the organizers and editors Heather Dubbeldam and Lola Sheppard. The participants, contributors, and sponsors can all be proud of creating an essential guide to the Canadian architectural landscape, and one that will continue to offer insight for generations to come.

Any jury or selection committee develops its own culture as the proceedings evolve, forging, as it matures, attitudes that come to frame its perspectives and choices. This year, the debate did not delve into what is or is not Canadian, or what comprises the avant-garde. Instead, in a context of comprehensive pluralism, the jury negotiated a wide spectrum of methodologies and metrics in the generation of meaning. These multiple tendencies of process and product evidence a robust and energetic operative milieu in Canada.

Many of this year's architectural practices seemed at ease with notions of collaborative firm organizations; collectives that, at times, bridged geographical and political borders, not merely as a necessity, but as a clear investment in internationalism and its perceived benefits. For example, WE-DESIGNS.ORG, with a pool of contributors that spans two continents, propagated a modus operandi of fluid knowledge exchange in the generation of its projects. Other firms created interdisciplinary teams that set the stage for more holistic design strategies, perhaps as a reflection of the small-scale, "found" quality of the commissions, but more likely because of an explicit desire to understand a problem in all its complexities.

Much of the design work was initiated as urban experiments: work that explored opportunities within density, multiple and overlapped programs, and complex adjacencies. A case in point—studio junction's Courtyard House—pursues infill housing through the conversion of a mid-block warehouse. The project's limitations meant the architects investigated a residential courtyard typology, with the material and tectonic logic to facilitate the transition from industrial context to residential space.

With a nod to commissions that fall "under the radar" of more established practices, and a desire to engage the built environment in a comprehensive manner, many projects were conceived as interventions in the public realm. This interdisciplinary context is characterized by the fertile overlap of architecture, urban design, landscape architecture, and public art. *Trop de bleu* by Olivier Bourgeois engages the landscape on the Magdalen Islands as a frame and social catalyst, while TBA's design for an amphitheatre deftly condenses its program as a sheltering roof that activates and defines its public space while recuperating usable landscape within the design of a green roof.

The contemporary interest in material manipulations towards effect and spatial complexity, often facilitated through a digital platform, certainly characterized a number of submitted projects. The OMS Stage walls by 5468796 Architecture were crafted into performative surfaces that catch and transform light, while activating both the park as a public beacon and the interior as a social condenser. PUBLIC's pavilion for the University of British Columbia features taut, folded surfaces that frame and define a space of engagement while its material and tectonic neutrality allows a subtle reading of the interplay of west coast light and water.

Based on a perhaps less topical research trajectory, but one that is definitely more entrenched within a Canadian architectural tradition, the cultivation of meaning through tectonic crafting was also evident in the projects. Omas's Urban Carriage House in New York weaves a complex architecture linking found, existing heritage fabric with contemporary habitation through skillfully crafted steel, glass, and wood insertions. Similarly, the de la Congrégation Residence, by _naturehumaine, realizes conceptual intention through tectonic, material, and colour juxtaposition.

Also part of the well-worn path of Canadian architectural production, several projects played off different guises of modernism, primarily as an exploration of the idea of abstraction and formal reduction. In a number of cases, formal reduction was the design strategy that contextualized the vernacular within the contemporary. Atelier Kastelic Buffey's Maison Glissade, in Collingwood, Ontario, wraps its simply organized program within a precise geometric skin revealing the iconic image of *house*, while Alec Brown's essay in minimalism, within the 350-year-old context of Lunenburg, distills the Cape Cod type into a sublime formal negotiation. In other projects, modernism's formal neutrality was the precondition to an architecture of the senses. The Nadège Patisserie, for example, by Toronto's nkArchitect , strips away any embellishment and leaves an edited interplay of displayed goods, aromas, and the consumer.

Whether the emergent practices' work offered insights into the development of new architectural trajectories or evidenced skill in situating projects within existing means of design production, the curatorial committee found an engaging and inclusive future for Canadian architecture. Congratulations again to all Twenty + Change contributors.

Marc Boutin
August 2011

2011 Curatorial Committee

Marc Boutin is the founder of The Marc Boutin Architectural Collaborative Inc. in Calgary, a research-based critical practice with an inter-disciplinary approach to design through the synthesis of art, architecture, urban design, and landscape architecture. The work of the firm has been recognised by national and international awards, competition wins, exhibitions, and publications, including the 2002 Canada Council Prix de Rome. Marc is a professor at the Faculty of Environmental Design at the University of Calgary, teaching architecture and urban design studios in the graduate architecture program. His teaching there has been recognized by many university teaching and research awards.

Renée Daoust is a principal of the firm Daoust Lestage Inc., an architecture and urban design firm in Montreal concerned with design at every scale, from the city to the object. The firm has been recognized with numerous provincial, national and international urban design and architecture awards. Renée is a member of the CCA Development Committee in Montreal, and has played a critical role as a member of the master planning team for Ryerson University in Toronto. In recent years she has served as a member of the Toronto Waterfront Design Review Panel and as President of the Board of the Festival international des Jardins de Métis.

Miyoko Ohtake is an editor at Dwell Media in San Francisco, California. She writes and edits articles for *Dwell* and *Dwell.com* about modern architecture and design, with specific interests in sustainable building, backyards and green spaces, and the intersection of food and design. Ohtake studied architecture at the University of Toronto before earning a master's degree in journalism from the S.I. Newhouse School of Public Communications at Syracuse University. She has also written for *Wired* and *Newsweek*, among others.

Larry Wayne Richards is Professor Emeritus and former Dean in the John H. Daniels Faculty of Architecture, Landscape, and Design at the University of Toronto. Previously he was Director of the Waterloo School of Architecture. He is an accomplished and prolific curator, writer, editor, critic, and professional advisor for design competitions. Prof. Richards has edited and written numerous books and authored over fifty articles published in journals such as *Architecture New York*, *Domus*, *Canadian Architect*, *Canadian Art*, *INSITE*, *Azure*, and *Parachute*. He has received numerous awards, including a national Award of Excellence (Advocate Award) from the Royal Architectural Institute of Canada. Since 2009 Richards has been Artistic Director of Toronto-based WORKshop, Inc.

Talbot Sweetapple is a partner at MacKay-Lyons Sweetapple Architects in Halifax, where he concentrates on medium to large scale public architecture projects which have won numerous awards and appeared in many international publications. Talbot is an Adjunct Professor at Dalhousie University's Faculty of Architecture where he teaches design and technology studios. He has also taught at Syracuse University, the University of Arkansas and in 2004, along with Brian Mackay-Lyons, was appointed to the Ruth and Norman Moore Chair at Washington University at St. Louis.

Introduction

Twenty + Change is a biennial exhibition and publication series dedicated to promoting the work of emerging Canadian design practices in the fields of architecture, landscape architecture and urban design. The Twenty + Change publication—a yearbook of sorts—serves to take the pulse of design interests amongst emerging Canadian practices. Emerging firms represent a valuable barometer of current design sensibilities across the country as their approach tends to be tactical: they take on smaller or unusual commissions, at times even initiating their own client groups or pursuing self-generated projects. Twenty + Change's mandate, fundamentally, is to disseminate the work of young firms who are starting to make their mark in the field, and to offer them visibility in a national forum.

The last edition of Twenty + Change was launched in 2009; and while a few firms reappear in the 2011 Twenty + Change 03 edition, for the most part a new group of young designers has come to the fore. Following a national call for submissions, the work was selected by a curatorial committee comprised of prominent educators, writers and practitioners from across the country. Firms from eleven cities in eight provinces submitted their work; nineteen were chosen, both for their practice approach and for the strength of their submitted projects. Selected firms were asked to provide a practice profile and project descriptions, allowing the book to fully represent the many design voices of the collection.

Prior to the launch of Twenty + Change 03, one of the initial tasks was to establish a clear definition of an "emerging" practice. It was decided that one qualification should be that selected firms were ten years old or less —recognizing the time it takes, particularly in North America, to launch and develop a practice. The curatorial committee also debated the question of how Twenty + Change should recognize design excellence; formal and tectonic innovation, new models of practice, the degree of risk-taking, and sustainable approaches were all ultimately taken into consideration.

Canadian architecture has historically focused largely on the exploration of craft, regionalism, and relationship to site, and the new generation appears to be continuing this legacy. The primacy of contextualism is another strong driver in many projects. As Will Jones suggests in his essay, clients and designers in Canada often have more conservative tastes and less appetite for conspicuous display and provocation than is the case in other countries. The ideas of mid-twentieth-century theorists, such as Kenneth Frampton's "critical regionalism" and Christian Norberg Schulz's *genius loci*, are still remarkably influential in much of the work. This is undoubtedly due both to the power of the Canadian landscape and to the continued search for Canadian identity in most cultural arenas, the discipline of architecture being no exception.

A number of projects chosen for Twenty + Change 03 explore and engage the public realm in meaningful ways, through temporary or permanent public installations or through projects that offer a fresh approach to urban living. Despite, or perhaps because of, the modest means and scope of most of these projects, they develop highly effective interventions to activate public spaces and landscapes in inventive, even whimsical, ways.

Multidisciplinarity is another recurring ambition presented in the practice profiles. Many of the firms offer graphic design, branding, signage, furniture design, and more in their portfolio of skills and work. This is in step with a current larger discourse on architecture, which seeks a return to a more comprehensive vision of the profession. Whether this return to an expanded role for the profession in the construction industry is driven by design ambition, or reflects an attempt to hold or reclaim territory rapidly being ceded to other professionals, one wonders, as these firms evolve, what type of commissions they will court in light of these ambitious beginnings. The desire—or need—to be multidisciplinary is perhaps most acute in young design firms, who, in the interest of getting work, are often required to be nimble, to experiment, and to take on diverse roles.

For many architects, their early years in the profession were a fertile time of testing nascent ideas and positions (and provoking the public around them). Seminal early projects such as Loos's American Bar in Vienna, Venturi's mother's house, or Arthur Erickson's west-coast houses, all served as testing grounds and provocations. The firms selected for Twenty + Change 03 are all, in their own way, testing positions. We encourage them to continue pushing and testing their ideas, developing their work, and through that work developing a discourse, within the discipline and amongst the public, that will be supportive of the built environment.

Heather Dubbeldam
Lola Sheppard

Emerging Ecologies

Peter Sampson

Le Corbusier was twenty-six when he conceptualized the "Domino house," a design that anticipated much of Europe's post-war reconstruction, years before the end of WWI. When he was thirty, Walter Gropius, along with an equally young Adolf Meyer, oversaw the completion of the seminal modernist Fagus Werk in Germany. At thirty-four, Rem Koolhaas published *Delirious New York*, announcing himself not as an emergent architect, but as an accomplished cultural critic who was about to reposition the path of postmodern idealism. In other fields, John Lennon was forty years old when he was murdered, and only twenty-nine when he and Yoko Ono held their "Give Peace a Chance" bed-in. Billie Holiday was twenty-four when she recorded her indelible rendition of the protest anthem, "Strange Fruit." Martin Luther King Jr. was assassinated at thirty-nine, and Mary Wollstonecraft was thirty-four when she wrote the feminist manifesto, *A Vindication of the Rights of Women* in 1792.

All of them young; all of them innovative amidst a cultural sea change. Not the only struggling artists facing uncertain futures, they were the ones who emerged because they were able to look forward, construct change, transform thinking, and lead reform. Beyond anything else, they rose to prominence by reshaping the ideologies, the practices, and the culture of their time. We are fascinated with the emergent practice, whether in music, literature, politics, or architecture, because through it we witness history in the making. Today's sea change is at once cultural and physical. Emerging ecologies that are the product of vast changes in the global habitat will certainly have profound impacts on the livelihoods, cultures, and politics of nations; on climate and weather patterns, and on the evolution of responsive technologies — all on a scale not yet fully realized. Practice amidst such global and local ecologies is uncharted territory for all architects.

Awards programs directed toward youth can be precise in their search for the best of what is emerging today. Especially for Canada, young on the world stage, Twenty + Change has positioned itself to focus on specific accomplishments in the landscape of new work, and to encourage us to ask what leadership role Canadian practice will assume. All too often, *emergence* in these coming-of-age parties has to do not with youth but with—*age*. The prestigious ar+d Awards for Emerging Architects, now in their thirteenth year, restrict the concept to a certain age group. "The age limit of 45 has been chosen on the basis that many emerging architects are unable to realize designs or develop an original vision before that time, whether because of the long education and training period, or because of lack of opportunity." Despite the exuberance of this and other "emerging firms" events, the ar+d exhibition highlights a troubling undertone that many young architects encounter in the field: prominence is reserved for those with experience.

What definition of emergence do we want to celebrate: growing up, or the transformation of practice as it moves towards new ideas for the time? Is it that the work looks as accomplished as that of a more seasoned firm, or that it challenges architectural approaches to contemporary conditions or critically dissects the status quo? Twenty + Change is positioned to attempt a definition in the coming years, encouraging its audience to speculate on ideas about the changing nature of Canadian practice, as seen through the eyes of younger firms looking to the future. A sample of questions is brewing in this year's collection. Winnipeg's 5468796 Architecture and Vancouver's RUF Project engage questions of density and affordability in our changing cities, McMinn + Janzen Studio and Atelier Kastelic Buffey test materiality and ecological approaches to place and construction, Omas and Alec Brown Architect provoke dialogues between competing histories of architecture and place. Being young is risky enough in a business that promotes and rewards experience. The critical objective for a publication like Twenty + Change is to establish a forum for ideas that challenge the authority of experience.

ar+d's portrayal of young architects grappling with practice, not yet experienced enough to compete against more seasoned firms for big contracts, might be relevant in larger cities where all too many firms must compete for a diminishing number of opportunities, and a track record for success trumps youth. But in this year's Twenty + Change, work emerging from smaller urban centres demonstrates that fuller opportunities do exist, and that provocative work is evolving that challenges the photogenic restaurants and houses that fit a more conventional notion of *young practices in larger centres*. A spirit of inventiveness over conformity, and questioning over obedience, seems acutely present in the work emerging from the Maritimes and the Prairies; places where the power of the status quo is perhaps less formidable. Here, architecture's relationship with the ecologies from which it emerges is fresh.

If emergence is not only about coming into prominence but also about constantly investigating new modes of practice, then there are broader ways to discuss emergent architecture. In the numerous publications featuring young architects, successes are celebrated as the thing itself.

We talk often of the difficulties young architects face in finding a voice, getting published, or winning their first big contract. We talk little about how their practice is preparing to evolve into a challenging future, and even less about the idea that emergence itself is at the core of all architectural practice, where ideas are at once relevant, radical, evolving, global, and perceptible to a wider audience than ourselves. And we do not talk at all about seasoned firms that continue to "emerge"—architects who, rather than just keeping up, anticipate the rapid transformations of technology, building science, project management, and climate through their work and ultimately through the way they practice.

The relevant question is how we collectively evolve as a profession struggling to maintain relevance in the face of rapidly mutating ecologies. The perspective of youth forces us to reflect on what it is that we are emerging *towards*. Many of the works in this year's Twenty + Change begin to highlight the importance of innovation, discipline, leadership, and the exciting yet complicated task of staying emergent in emerging times. When Le Corbusier entered his recycled version of the *plan voisin* for the Hauptstadt Berlin competition later in his life—a point by which his emergence was presumably secure—he lost the competition, and some might say his relevance to the age. Prominence in architecture—that thing towards which emergence tends—is fleeting if not cultivated by continually re-emerging and youthful approaches to the changing conditions of practice.

Artist, Activist and Guardian

Will Jones

The construction industry is considered by many economists to be an important early indicator of the health and wealth of a city, a nation, or the world as a whole. As financial confidence begins to course through society, individuals and organizations look to expand, and building begins. Similarly, when money is tight, the first thing to slow is construction.

Architecture is inherently linked to this cycle of boom and bust. But while the work of contractors and the economic health of a society can be assessed purely by volume, the design of buildings—the architecture of the moment—is a different kind of indicator, demonstrating not only the extent of commissions available but also the emotional well-being of a society, a nation, or the world.

In both the upward and downward cycles of our roller-coaster global economy, architects can choose to design purely to get the work, or they can design with the long-term state of the economy and environment in mind. The choice is an interesting one and a look back at the most fêted designers of the last two decades tells of the extravagances and short-term dalliances that have dominated the architectural world, when perhaps we should have been thinking ahead and working towards a more sustainable future.

Frank Gehry, Zaha Hadid, Jürgen H. Mayer, Daniel Libeskind, Future Systems—the list of architects vying for the glamour job and the moniker of "starchitect" is long and international, and to give these architects their due, their designs are imaginative and dramatic. Their buildings are to our cities what pinstripe tailoring and shoulder pads were to fashion in the opulent 1980s.

But what do these extravagant architectural gestures offer the world after a global financial meltdown? How might architecture respond to new economic, social and environmental challenges? Here's the crux of the architect's conundrum: architects have control over their designs, be they large or small; they are responsible for how buildings get built in our cities and countryside. But architects must also be accountable for the impact that their designs have on the world: they must take responsibility for their work, now and for years to come.

And so, it is exciting to see that the studios chosen to be featured in Twenty + Change 03 are actively confronting these issues, and creating designs that respond to and will benefit our current socio-economic state; they are researching the emotional impact of architecture; they are practising environmentally and endeavouring to engage the wider public in their work; they are embracing the responsibilities that are thrust upon them.

Contrasting examples of architecture/design with an emotional effect can be seen in Acre Architects' bus stop installation and the Camp at Cabot Beach by Idea Tank Design Collective. Both projects give joy, but achieve it in very different ways. Similarly, the public urinal designed by Matthew Soules Architecture will make people smile, but its design is serious—a solution to functional, aesthetic, and public safety issues conveniently curled into an abstract sculpture that you can pee behind too.

Designing responsibly for the environment and community should be a cornerstone of all twenty-first-century architecture, be it a private home or a cultural edifice. Centre Village, by the surprisingly named 5468796 Architecture, takes inspiration and reference from European high-density housing. This contrasts with much traditional North American residential architecture but bodes well for the future, both environmentally and economically. In addition, the practice states that it is attempting to create "true community," an important goal in today's ever more isolating, digitally driven society.

It is good to see that people matter in Canadian architecture and refreshing that young practices are not simply vying to design the extravagant and outlandish in their quest to become successful. But why not? Talking to Canadian firms, one realizes that while clients do not lack resources and have just as much ambition as their international counterparts, the nation as a whole is relatively orthodox in its tastes: there is a cultural disdain of the kind of extrovert displays of wealth that can be seen in China, the Middle East and even western Europe. This conservative nature can be frustrating for young architects yearning to experiment and spread their creative wings but ultimately it is a beneficial constraint; one that pushes Canadian practices to design brilliantly within tight parameters, be they physical, financial or cultural.

As such, the examples of new Canadian architecture in Twenty + Change 03 look to create site-specific, non-disposable architecture that is integrated with its landscape and community. And the practitioners utilize the most advanced technology while working with traditional materials and creating designs imbued with historical ideals.

This cross-section of architects and designers is an indication that we can be optimistic about the future of the profession in Canada and the built environment at large. Some of the studios featured here will go on to design and build the architectural behemoths of tomorrow. They will be the firms solicited by cultural organizations and corporate giants who want to make an architectural splash. However, while the Frank Gehrys and Zaha Hadids of this world have thrived in recent years, in a culture of excess, it is clear that the architects cutting their teeth today in a world of economic and environmental constraints will remember their responsibilities, and seek to be not only architectural artists but also environmental activists and social guardians for the built environment in which we live.

**Twenty + Change 03
Projects**

5468796 Architecture Inc.

Winnipeg, Manitoba

5468796 Architecture Inc. is a Winnipeg-based
studio established in 2007. The firm is composed of
twelve committed young professionals, representing
a diverse cross-section of design knowledge. In its
four years of existence, the office has gained national
and international recognition through numerous
awards, publications, and competitions, both in
Canada and abroad. Each project is first defined by
a set of constraints, which invariably open the door
to a unique and comprehensive array of possibilities.
The office then focuses its energy in determining an
uncompromising approach to the design. Beyond
designing built work, 5468796 Architecture makes
design advocacy an ongoing pursuit through critical
practice, seeking opportunities both to enhance
design debate among practitioners and to promote
public awareness of architecture in Winnipeg.

5468796 Architecture, in collaboration with Jae-Sung
Chon, was selected by a national juried competition
as Canada's official entry at the 2012 Venice Biennale
in Architecture. The Migrating Landscapes exhibition
explores the settling/unsettling dynamic of
im/migration, acting as a forum for Canadian
designers to investigate and expose the
unique manifestations of cultural memory that
pervade our country. The project, framed as a
national competition in which young Canadian
practitioners will contribute their responses to
our multidimensional topography, will travel
from British Columbia to Nova Scotia, before
it reaches its final destination in Italy.

OMS Stage
Winnipeg, MB

"The Cube" is an open-air performance venue set against the backdrop of historic warehouses in Winnipeg's Exchange District. The design, commissioned after an invited competition, recognizes that the stage only functions as such during a very limited season, and offers alternative opportunities for use during the rest of the year. In its final form, the stage is articulated as a multi-functional environment that shifts from a vibrant performance space to an ephemeral, glowing, interactive pavilion and focal point.

The outer shell of the stage is a dynamic membrane composed of diamond-shaped aluminum extrusions strung together to form a flexible curtain that can be drawn back to reveal the stage and structure within. The retracted skin in turn becomes a draped and undulating ceiling landscape, providing a backdrop for performances and allowing adjustments to the stage's acoustics. When closed, the custom-built screen captures and refracts light or images to its outer surface, creating a unique pixel matrix. Programmable lighting shines onto the pixelated skin offering a space or surface for seasonally programmed interactive displays: a showcase available for use by local artists. In its closed position, the stage also accommodates small off-season gatherings and exhibitions within.

By focusing on year-round applications for the stage program, the team was motivated to develop a constituent part of the program (security, screen, canopy), into a new project feature. The skin thereby transcends its role as shell and takes on a new, performative role. The project also explores light as a material to be exploited in design—one that adds richness and depth rather than simply functional illumination.

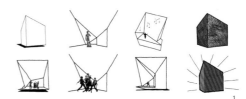

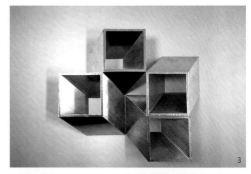

1   The Cube's programmatic possibilities
2   Individual aluminum extrusions that form a flexible curtain
3   A module composed of a series of four rotated aluminum extrusions
4   One state of changing lights during a music festival
5   Aerial view overlooking Old Market Square and King Street
6   View from behind the screen

5468796 Architecture Inc.

5

6

Centre Village
Winnipeg, MB

Centre Village is a twenty-five-unit housing co-op located on a small infill lot in Winnipeg's Central Park neighbourhood. The project strives to create a true community—a housing village—with modest means. The design is based on simple 8-by-12-foot modules organized along a central spine or "bar." The sizes of all rooms are based on European norms, more compressed than North American standard, yet still providing livable space and ultimately respecting the site density required by the business plan. Occasionally, the base module is replaced by a larger 14-by-12-foot unit that cantilevers off the main spine to expand the master bedroom or living room. Each of the upper units has its own rooftop patio, and second-storey units are accessed by exterior staircases.

While the housing spaces are minimal, the eight-foot "bar," or band, allows each unit to have views in multiple orientations, as well as cross-ventilation. The vibrant orange colour used both to define the ceiling plane in the space and to reflect light is pulled out of the living spaces through the window cowlings, which punch the interior space out of the building, capturing views and extending the perceived living spaces outdoors. A typical unit has eight or more windows, liberally scattered throughout to mediate the smaller interior and enlarge the sense of space and reflected light.

The mixture of standardized modules creates richness and variability on the site, generating a seemingly unorganized, yet carefully considered composition of one-, two-, three- and even four-bedroom homes. These bars of housing are arranged around two inner spaces accessible to all residents—a landscaped courtyard and an internal streetscape. These shared spaces are then connected to the broader neighbourhood, encouraging interaction and dialogue.

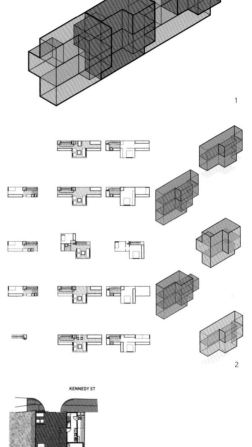

1

2

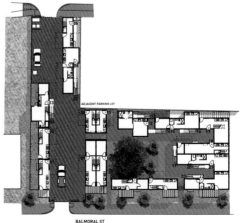

3

1 Example of Centre Village block with four intertwined units
2 Plans and axonometric drawings showing spatial adjacencies of rooms
3 Site plan of Centre Village development
4 View of communal courtyard
5 Secondary bedroom with a view overlooking Balmoral Street
6 Pattern of punched windows with orange cowlings
7 Balmoral Street elevation of Centre Village

5468796 Architecture Inc.

4

5

6

7

Acre Architects

Saint John, New Brunswick

When starting an architectural firm in a recession, one learns quickly that versatility and flexibility are key to survival. Acre Architects are finding that to be viable, a young practice must take risks and look for the opportunity in every challenge.

Stephen Kopp and Monica Adair lead the Acre and draw upon the expertise of the *acre collective*, a small group of gifted artists, landscape architects, writers and architects. The idea is simple: bring together the right team for the right project. The collective finds fresh ways to tackle projects and produce new outcomes. At the heart of each new endeavour is a collaborative spirit of playfulness and exploration.

After considering the question of where to set up shop, the Acre chose Saint John as its home. As a primary objective, the practice aims to promote a greater understanding of the role of contemporary architecture in shaping the culture and identity of New Brunswick. Acre's recently completed public art piece, *In transit*, constitutes their initial offering of engagement in this public realm.

Current Acre projects include two custom houses under construction, a small luxury ecological inn located in a remote part of Newfoundland, an apple orchard cider house, and a new home for a microbrewery in Fredericton, NB.

In Transit
Saint John, NB

We began in fog, against a concrete wall.
The silence of the missing element was deafening.
Where was the colour?

A ninety-minute bus ride in search of the missing element heightened our awareness of a ubiquitous language, one that spoke to us incessantly throughout our bus journey—MERGE, it said, and STOP, DANGER, YIELD, SLOW, TURN, EXIT. Surprisingly, coded traffic signs were the most striking source of colour along the roadway. Constantly reappearing, infallibly present when needed, their messages invested the road with meaning. Their bright colour and contrast conveyed explicit, unequivocal guidance.

The omnipresence of transit signs in our lives has given these colourful icons a cloak of invisibility. Habit means that we see them, but we do not see them. *In transit*, the new bus stop installation, challenges the viewer to bring the art of the roadway into conscious awareness and to reinterpret its meaning.

When familiarity is captured, it is transformed. With its use of the standardized traffic colours, print screen type, materiality, and the planar condition intrinsic to sign typology, *In transit* seeks to challenge the way we see our highways. It encourages the observer, contrary to the traffic sign's intended purpose, to consider its visual dimension. Grey is part of the collective psyche of Saint John, a city that fog knows well. And the colourlessness of the large wall of the city's bus terminal station offers the perfect contrast for a juxtaposed display of stylized colour.

In transit is composed of 85 unique aluminum panels (each two feet wide and 10 feet high), ten of which are sculpted into simple benches whose form was inspired by the simplicity of the bus seat. Anchored to the existing concrete retaining wall, the panels create a new landscape of colour that runs along this formerly derelict street.

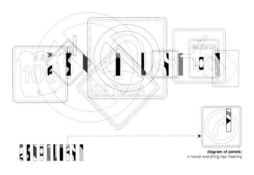

diagram of panels:
in transit everything has meaning

1

1   In transit - panel diagram
2   Bus stop seating
3   Bus terminal entrance
4   Competition rendering
5   In transit activated by car lights

2

Acre Architects

Alec Brown Architect

Halifax, Nova Scotia

Alec Brown Architect was founded in 2009. The practice has undertaken commercial, institutional, health care and residential projects. Alec Brown grew up in Nova Scotia, and attended the University of St. Andrews, Scotland, and the Technical University of Nova Scotia, graduating in 1993. He worked with McDowell+Benedetti in London and Studio Libeskind in Berlin before returning to Nova Scotia.

The firm's design approach emphasizes sensitivity, minimalism, and boldness. Meticulous details and simple materials are set within rigorously determined formal relationships. Elements can be at once harmonious and audacious. To this end, the office has completed a number of projects which involve the modernization of heritage buildings, allowing new and raw contemporary functional elements to co-exist with the richness of renewed original building fabric.

An ongoing area of research in the office is vernacular form and detail. This has entailed exploration of the rich building traditions in Nova Scotia, as well as studies of primitive types of dwellings in Britain, Italy, and Africa. Brown believes that an anthropological understanding of spatial configurations in cultures with a less overtly developed architecture can offer resonant sources for modern design projects.

Cross Passage House
Lunenburg, NS

Founded in 1753, the town of Lunenburg in Nova Scotia remains an outstanding intact example of British colonial town planning and historic architecture in North America. The Cross Passage House project is located on what was one of the last unbuilt lots within the UNESCO Lunenburg Old Town Heritage District. The design is an attempt to distill the archetypal three-quarter Cape Cod typology, investigating how and where heritage elements (mandated in this case) and minimalist formalism might coexist. To be consistent with the style, the eaves had to be utterly simple, low, and with minimal projection; to achieve this detail, a design was developed that had its own roof ventilation, drainage, and joist-bearing details.

The plan is informed by studies of an earlier antecedent to the colonial Cape Cod style, the seventeenth-century English cross-passage house. In this typology, the living quarters for human residents and domestic animals were under the same roof, divided by a passage running front to back, with a hearth as focal point in the open living space and a loft above. Modern open-plan design is in some ways more reminiscent of this earlier, primitive type of English dwelling than of its more recent colonial incarnations.

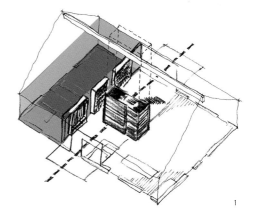

1

2

1   Axonometric parti sketch showing English cross-passage house layout
2   East elevation from adjacent historic cemetery
3   View from kitchen towards living area
4   Detail of large sliding doors of hearth element
5   Front elevation showing low eaves, without overhang or gutter

Atelier Kastelic Buffey Inc.
Toronto, Ontario

AKB, founded in 2004, is an integrated architecture and interior design studio based in Toronto, under the direction of Robert Kastelic and Kelly Buffey.

Kastelic and Buffey believe that architecture and interiors fundamentally shape the way we experience the world, and that a coherent relationship between exterior and interior makes the experience of place honest and profound. With this in mind, they aim for a clarity of vision to define all of their projects, creating buildings that are both engaging and functional. They design with a modernist's approach to order, integrity, and grace; a poet's desire for nature, warmth, and humanity; and an environmentalist's sustainable and long-term vision. Their commitment to contemporary design is manifested in spaces that unfold and resonate across many scales and over time.

The practice works collaboratively to explore how their clients' needs can find expression and how they can experience new relationships with their environment. Each project is unique, as they draw an understanding from the site, program, and context, and examine methods to optimize ergonomics and address environmental concerns. By researching the data, theories, and precedents underpinning a project, the team develops a series of questions that lead to concentrated and creative solutions.

Maison Glissade
Collingwood, ON

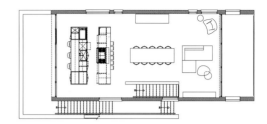

At the base of a ski resort hill, this barn-like structure is modest yet dynamic, with an iconic form that gestures towards the mountain slope. The design was conceived for a family of five to live simply and comfortably together within a small footprint, and to create experiences that evolve with season and time.

Efficient and functional bedrooms, bathrooms, and a large mudroom on the ground floor encourage users to congregate on the second floor within an open-concept living room, dining room and kitchen. Under a gabled roof, the interior walls and ceiling mimic the exterior profile, opening at each end to offer picturesque views of the countryside. To maximize the openness of this space, a steel frame was integrated into the structure to enable a continuous expanse, unimpeded by exposed beams or dividing walls.

1

By shifting and slightly protruding the second storey, AKB created an exterior façade that clearly expresses a connection between exterior and interior proportions. By day the project emphasizes its exterior form and, from the inside, views of the surrounding landscape; but by night its physical structure seems to dematerialize as the illuminated interior is revealed.

Built within the existing footprint of a previous residence, the chalet minimized site disturbance. Interior finish selections are all natural and ecologically friendly, and the exterior cladding consists of western red cedar, a renewable resource. The interior is warmed throughout by hydronic radiant in-floor heating. Optimal natural light conditions reduce the need for artificial lighting, resulting in lower energy consumption. Large, operable windows transform the second floor into a breezeway, with maximum natural air flow. Extensive plantings of indigenous trees and grasses make the chalet appear to grow out of the land. Long, soft grasses emphasize the strength of the chalet's volume and enhance the project's tranquility.

1   Above: second floor plan; below: ground floor plan
2   Chalet at dusk, view from field
3   Second floor dining room, living room and front deck
4   Chalet by day, view from street

Atelier Kastelic Buffey Inc.

Chevalier Morales Architectes
Montréal, Québec

Stephan Chevalier and Sergio Morales strive to create contemporary architecture that responds not only to the client but also to the community and the environment. Understanding the intrinsic aesthetic qualities of materials, qualities of light, and the form of spaces, they are equally conscious of the needs, ideas, and comfort of those who will live or work in the buildings they conceive for them. Chevalier Morales believes that environmental awareness is one of an architect's fundamental responsibilities, and that concerns about global warming and reduction of pollution should be addressed wherever possible through innovative building design.

Twentieth- and twenty-first century values like *multiplicity*, *exactitude*, *lightness*, and *quickness*, as outlined by Italo Calvino in his *Six Memos for the Next Millennium*, are part of the Chevalier Morales vision, as are the concepts of *movement*, *territory*, and *identity*. They believe that a design that is created with attention to these fundamental concepts can embody the spirit of place, and begin to influence the wider community. Generalists in an industry where specialization is common, the partners believe that their role as architects is similar to that of an orchestra conductor: coordinating, leading, and gathering people together while making sure that the end result will be as rigorous, as coherent, and as aesthetically pleasing as it was when first envisioned during the early stages of design.

Spa at Nuns' Island

Montréal, QC

Outdoor spas are becoming more popular, perhaps replacing traditional amusement parks such as the emblematic Coney Island in New York City or La Ronde on St. Helen's Island in Montreal. Instead of experiencing sensational kinetic thrills, visitors are treated to peaceful interludes of relaxation and stress relief, where the body is massaged, soothed, pampered, and cared for. Some thrills remain, however—for example, passing from a steaming hot bath to an ice-cold one, for which a small amount of courage is still required.

Chevalier Morales's treatment of this new type of playground for the body offers a sensitive contemporary design. Three separate buildings are located on manmade topography and anchored into the sloping terrain at different levels, looking out onto the lake at the south end of Nuns' Island in Montreal. The principal building houses a reception area, administrative offices, a bistro, massage rooms, and change rooms. Two smaller buildings house a Turkish bath and a Finnish sauna, each with its own solarium. The compound is organized around a network of exterior baths that are positioned to take advantage of the beautiful views over the lake, and to offer varied and intimate discoveries to users. The landscape here becomes an essential part of the experience of the place. Covered in grey clay brick—a Nuns' Island requirement—and white wood, the buildings exude calm and serenity. Brass elements like the unusual sculptures, gargoyles, and interior furniture make visual reference to the hidden systems of pipes that are responsible for the experiences that the spa provides.

At night, the neon and LED lights and flaming torches illuminate the surreal décor touched by pinks and light blues, evoking childhood memories of amusement parks. When snow falls in winter, the lighting produces even more striking, ethereal effects.

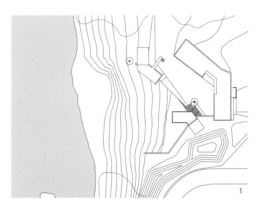

1

2

1   Site plan
2   Outdoor bath
3   Overall view of spa buildings at dusk
4   Outdoor bistro
5   Turkish bath access
6   Main interior circulation

Chevalier Morales Architectes

3

4

5

6

Great Lake Studio

Toronto, Ontario

To visit the wilderness is to participate in some of the oldest human traditions. Warming ourselves by fires, marvelling at the night sky, exploring the silent depths of a forest, we are immersed in an expansive mystery. In the wilderness we come into contact with essential aspects of our humanity: sensuality, spirituality, mystery, and myth.

Great Lake Studio is a Toronto-based architecture practice founded by Rick Galezowski, who has collaborated with several of Canada's leading, award-winning architects. His work at these firms has received multiple awards and is included in the permanent collection of the Museum of Modern Art.

Between 2000 and 2006, Galezowski travelled around the world on a bicycle. During this period he lived in a small nylon tent, under open skies, in all environmental conditions, in some of the most remote and diverse wildernesses on the planet. This adventure, with its modest comforts and small rituals, was experienced against the profoundly contrasting background of vast landscapes and wild climates. It confirmed his deep respect for the natural world, which strongly influences the work of Great Lake Studio.

Temagami Wilderness Camp
Temagami, ON

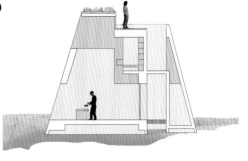

Temagami Wilderness Camp translates Galezowski's experience of living outdoors for an extended period into architecture. Located on a rugged slope of granite shield in the boreal forest of Northern Ontario, the camp is a seasonal shelter from which parties may venture into the surrounding wilderness on foot or by canoe. Programmatic requirements were minimal: a place to gather, dine, and sleep for up to eight people, a water pump, and a fireplace. In contrast, creating a close engagement with the wilderness for modern adventure-seekers was a more complex and ambitious task. Inspiration was found in traditional shelters as disparate as yurts, igloos, tents, and native longhouses; each of these models offers an example of human ingenuity protecting a fragile and at times tenuous existence amid the sublime beauty and potential terror of elemental forces. Paradoxically, it is this vulnerability that confers the most exciting and sensual experience of nature. The notion of managed vulnerability was a defining theme of the project; balancing shelter against exposure to the elements.

A pair of tapered, overlapping shells establishes an enclosure in the forest. Between these shells, a sheltered "veranda" both separates and connects two enclosures, a "bunkhouse" and a "bath house," dissolving distinctions between interior space and the outdoors. The bunkhouse's sliding partitions allow further management of the indoor-outdoor relationship: a mild rain shower may require closing one area, whereas in truly ferocious weather it may be necessary to batten down the entire system. A sleeping loft in the rafters provides a basic, functional experience of shelter, while a rooftop observatory offers exactly the opposite—a thrilling lookout for surveying the landscape, stargazing, or experiencing a storm. Binding all these together, a manifold structure of deep vertical louvres acts as diffuser of light, capturing the traverse of celestial bodies above and lanterns from within.

1

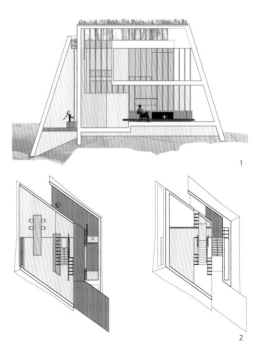

2

1   Sections: a vertical terrain inviting playful exploration
2   Lower and upper plans: horizontal landscape of enclosure / exposure
3   A lantern in the forest with podium raised to the stars
4   Bunkhouse communal space in open configuration
5   Shell structure resting lightly on the rock slope

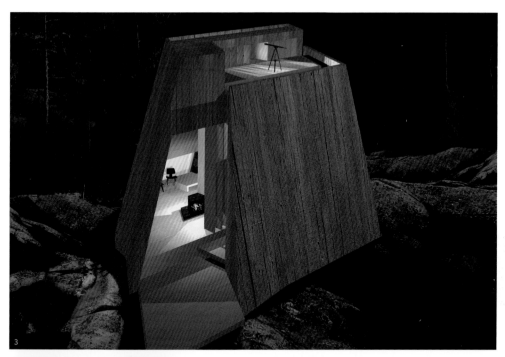

Idea Tank Design Collective
Toronto, Ontario

Idea Tank Design Collective is a group of five designers - Clayton Blackman, Andrew Choptiany, Mark Erickson, Matthew Kennedy, and Sam Lock - who met at Dalhousie University and found a deep, shared interest in craft and design. The team has a diverse set of skills that extend beyond architecture to construction, graphic design, photography, and fine art. Believing in the power of collaboration, they find that their best ideas for each project are the result of working collectively to achieve one goal: meaningful design of the highest quality.

Design methodology always begins with site visits and conversations with those who will use the building. Concepts from these first-hand experiences, distilled into sketch models and hand drawings, are pushed rigorously through development using varied tools, from 3-D computer modeling to scaled mockups. With a special interest in craft and a passion for construction, the team is involved through the building phase of every project.

Idea Tank is deeply committed to social responsibility. Using local, durable, and environmentally sustainable materials, they strive to create beautiful spaces that will have a positive impact on the lives of those who experience the completed work.

Camp at Cabot Beach
Malpeque, PEI

The Camp at Cabot Beach is designed and built to address the needs of children living in families that have been affected by chronic illness or disability. Every year, they get the chance to escape by spending a week with other kids in similar situations. A Nova Scotian charity was given a plot of land on the north coast of Prince Edward Island near Malpeque Harbour and Cabot Beach Provincial park, and wanted to create a permanent camping facility. Having spent a summer as counsellors at the camp, Idea Tank's designers had first-hand experience of what the campers needed in a building and were excited to provide a new space for camp activities.

The first design move was to create a camp "bubble" apart from the surrounding community, in a safe space defined by an existing ring of trees and a new linear building—a place where children could thrive and explore. The buildings, consisting of washrooms, kitchen, and dining hall, have slanted roofs allowing daylighting and passive ventilation, with insulated southern walls providing a reprieve from the summer sun and the noise of the community. The northern wall of the dining hall is transparent, offering a view of the activity in the field beyond, while also creating meaningful indoor space.

The buildings use traditional materials and techniques of the area: locally harvested dimensional lumber and cedar shingle cladding, and simply tilted durable metal roofs echoing the industrial barns of the area, all hovering over the ground on more than 125 wooden posts. Touching the ground lightly, the buildings' design allows for the possibility of disassembly and relocation if the camp needs to move to another site in the future.

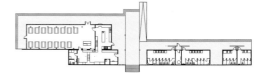

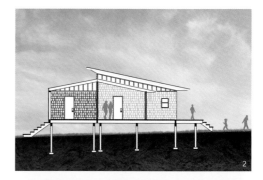

1   Plan of camp complex
2   Section through entry boardwalk showing the dining hall
3   Rafter detail with polycarbonate clerestory and cedar shingle cladding
4   South elevation drawing
5   North elevation at night with dining hall at right
6   View of the dining hall from south-west at dusk

Idea Tank Design Collective

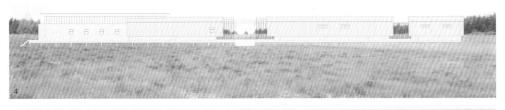

4

5

6

Matthew Soules Architecture Inc.
Vancouver, British Columbia

Matthew Soules Architecture (MSA) works on
diverse projects, from the very small to the very
large, and in contexts ranging from the dense
and urban to the wild and remote. Through the
combined activities of research, writing, teaching,
and design practice, MSA explores an array of
topics including the large potential of small-scale
public space insertions, the experiential and
performative possibilities of artificial ecologies,
the relationship between ideology and space, and
emergent forms of density. Completed built work to
date includes Harbour Centre Dental in downtown
Vancouver, a warehouse-to-office conversion in
Vancouver's Strathcona neighbourhood, and a
public urinal in Victoria. Ongoing work includes
a large sports resort in the Cascade Mountains,
public bicycle infrastructure for the City of Victoria,
and a laneway house in Vancouver. Theoretical
speculations and texts have appeared in journals
such as *Praxis* and *Harvard Design Magazine* as
well as being exhibited at the Vancouver Art
Gallery. MSA has received numerous awards,
including the 2010 Emerging Firm Award from the
Architectural Institute of British Columbia. In all its
work, MSA resists universal solutions, signature
styles, and the myth of the architect's isolated
genius, instead aiming to produce architecture
that is highly practical, yet surprisingly radical.

Victoria Public Urinal

Victoria, BC

The Victoria Public Urinal seeks to reinvent the nineteenth-century European *pissoir* for twenty-first-century Victoria. The first urinal was built in 2010 and more installations are planned. The project responds to Victoria's rich built heritage by embracing its defining texture and ornament, but in a fresh manner. The repetition of standard steel pipes to create the urinal's privacy screen offers a new kind of abstract ornament that mixes history and the future.

The overall configuration and shape of the urinal is defined entirely by performance criteria. To fit into numerous public locations where space is a premium, it must be as compact as possible, hence the circular plan. To make it simple and highly durable it was necessary to avoid moving parts that always seem to break in high-use public settings—hence the "yin-yang" entry that allows privacy without a closing door. To be highly useable a public urinal needs to balance privacy, so people feel comfortable using it, with transparency to discourage unwanted activities and ensure safety. To this end, the undulating wave of the screen creates visibility at foot level, and the alternate pipe lengths offer visibility at eye level. The result is a simple and durable device that offers a new kind of intensification of the public domain.

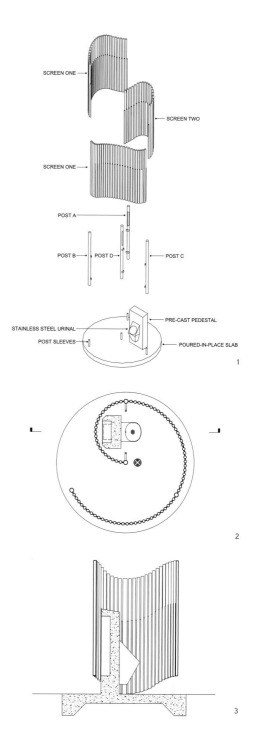

1   Exploded axonometric showing components
2   Plan drawing
3   Section drawing
4   Night view of entrance
5   Day view of full enclosure
6   Alternating pipe lengths offer visibility at eye level
7   Screen undulates to create visibility at foot level

Matthew Soules Architecture Inc.

4

5

6

McMinn + Janzen Studio

Toronto, Ontario

McMinn + Janzen Studio, based in Toronto, engages in architecture as a poetic and nuanced interpretation of program and context in both urban and extra-urban landscapes, in residential, institutional, and commercial contexts. The studio focuses on the potential of fabricated environments as an enhancement of cultural life in the city and its surroundings, with the intrinsic objective of efficient and responsible use of available resources in the short and long term. Melana Janzen is an OAA-registered architect and holds a Master of Architecture degree from the University of Waterloo. She writes periodically on topics in Canadian architecture for architectural journals and advocates for neighbourhood building, for the benefit of the city and also the future of her two small children. John McMinn has taught at schools of architecture in North America and Europe, and currently teaches at the University of Waterloo. He holds degrees from the Architectural Association in London, UK, and McGill University. He is a writer and curator of architectural exhibitions, focusing on the cultural dimensions of sustainable architecture from a critical regionalist perspective.

CP Harbour House

Big Bay, ON

The CP Harbour House is a vacation home for two Toronto families on the shores of Georgian Bay north of Owen Sound, Ontario. Overlooking offshore islands and the limestone cliffs of the Bruce Peninsula, it appears to hover above a small harbour marina where sailboats and motorboats are kept by residents of nearby island cottages.

The building is an assembly of four discrete enclosures linked by an expansive deck and roof. Double-storey serviced cabins are flanked by smaller guest bunkies, providing autonomy to the two families' separate quarters; one intensely social, the other with a focus on play-scapes for young children. The interior areas are modest and tightly planned for snug winter accommodation, but in summer the house expands, with a greatly enlarged outdoor living spaces under the sweeping reach of the roof. The totemic, temple-like quality of the post-and-beam structure provides a flexible armature for hanging seats, swings, beds, and lanterns, amplifying both the social events and play functions of the program.

Careful site integration based on building orientation and configuration was planned for a net-zero carbon footprint, which was also achieved through optimized passive heating, cooling, and ventilation, wood-burning heat, and a large photovoltaic array. Available local materials and artisanal production methods were used, including earthen floors of sand and clay quarried from a neighbour's site, and locally harvested cedar decking and siding, manufactured by a nearby Amish community's horse-drawn milling operation. Other sustainable products include bamboo plywood cabinets, mineral-wool and soya-based insulation, salvaged thermal glazing and slate countertops from billiard tables, reused slate flooring, and fabric for balustrades and privacy screens sourced from a terminated garment factory. The photovoltaic array will provide energy for electric vehicles when the market provides them, reducing the carbon cost of travel to and from the city.

1   Conceptual diagram
2   Floor plans
3   North guest bunkie
4   Living / dining area
5   Central exterior common area

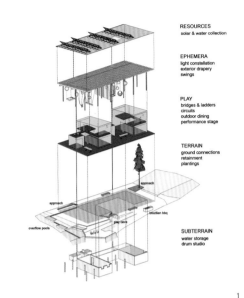

RESOURCES
solar & water collection

EPHEMERA
light constellation
exterior drapery
swings

PLAY
bridges & ladders
circuits
outdoor dining
performance stage

TERRAIN
ground connections
retainment
plantings

SUBTERRAIN
water storage
drum studio

1

GROUND FLOOR
1/16" = 1'-0"

SECOND FLOOR
1/16" = 1'-0"

2

McMinn + Janzen Studio

3

4

5

_naturehumaine [architecture+design]

Montréal, Québec

_naturehumaine is a Montreal-based architecture firm founded by Stéphane Rasselet and Marc-André Plasse. Their design process is always premised on the context and specific nature of each project. Their objective is to actualize the potentialities of the site, and to confer on it a unique and lively personality. The wide range of their work shows their curiosity and desire to explore the creative potential of each project: for them, architecture is not purely a self-reflective design gesture but a skilled response to a set of symbolic, economic, sociological, environmental, and cultural conditions. With their work, they wish to position architecture as a predominant force in the evolution of contemporary ideas and lifestyles.

De La Congrégation Residence

Montréal, QC

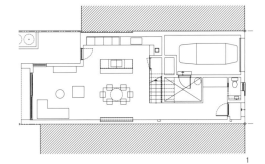

In the summer of 2008, the clients bought an empty lot on De La Congrégation Street, in the heart of the Pointe-St-Charles district in Montreal. They wanted to build a house that was as luminous and fluid as possible, with a continuous relationship to the exterior, south-oriented garden.

The concept of the house is based on a physical distinction between living space and work space. The interior volume is modulated through the introduction of a vertical spatial shear, which divides the house into two zones. This separation is marked by a double flight of stairs, a glass catwalk and a double-height source of indirect light. This is where all viewpoints converge: it is within this vertical aperture that the playful dynamic of the house is centred.

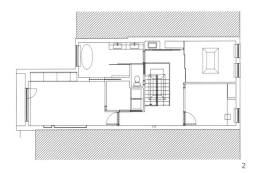

To enhance the quality of natural light within the house, the material palette was varied but neutral: a concrete floor on the ground floor; mostly white walls and kitchen cabinets with a few black accents; white oak used on the second floor, stairs and built-in furniture; natural steel used for the bookshelves and the handrail; and black slate for the bathroom and the kitchen wall.

The street façade is composed of dark brown brick accentuated by a series of recessed horizontal joints and Spanish cedar panels located in conjunction with the window layout. The articulation of the rear façade is formally conceived as a "coat collar", composed of black undulating steel panels that project from the roof line and upper walls, providing visual protection from the two adjacent neighbours. The ochre colour of the painted concrete panels on the rear façade creates a sense of drama in contrast with the sobriety of the street façade. The design responds to the strict constraints imposed by the city to keep the street face of the building subdued, and also achieves the desired goal of integrating the rear façade into Montreal's varied backyard architecture.

1   Ground floor plan
2   Second floor plan
3   Back façade
4   Stair and dining room
5   Second floor stair hall
6   Dining room and kitchen

St-Hubert Residence
Montréal, QC

The clients wished to enlarge their 800-square-foot bungalow by adding a second storey to the existing structure. However, the poor conditions of the foundations quickly proved this to be impossible. Instead, the architects studied the option of building an extension into the backyard. Two major constraints were encountered: a municipal prohibition against any construction higher than the existing roof, and the presence of rock at a depth of four feet below the surface, which would have made the construction of a basement very costly. Within these limitations, an unconventional and affordable solution was developed: compressing the design into numerous split levels created enough space for the desired rooms, with a stunning double-height dining room and a generous provision of natural light.

The first gesture was to lower the new dining room to the level of the exterior terrace and to link it with the kitchen and music room through a vast open space. Suspended above the dining room, a translucent reading cube emerges from the master bedroom. In addition, a light well ensures that direct sunlight reaches the dining room all day long. The kitchen is organized around an ample central counter island that becomes the focus of the social life in the house.

To meet the extremely tight budget, the selected building materials were deliberately left raw and untouched. The floor is covered with an antique waxed maple flooring; while fibrocement panels were used in the dining room. The interior roof structure of the existing house was left exposed and painted white to lighten up the spaces. The rear façade is covered with black pine planks combined with industrial corrugated steel sheeting, with an aluminum-zinc Galvalume finish.

The project plays in a subversive manner with the numerous constraints to produce a unique result. Simple and modest, the St-Hubert residence offers a rich living environment with generous and luminous spaces.

1   Longitudinal section
2   Ground floor plan
3   Dining room and translucent cube
4   Dining room and kitchen
5   Kitchen and central counter island
6   New rear façade

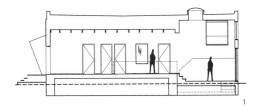

1

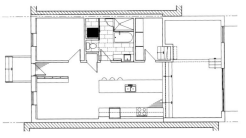

2

3

nkArchitect

Toronto, Ontario

nkA is an emerging practice whose design team members have backgrounds in architecture, design, and construction. Based in Toronto, this young studio focuses on a process of architecture that engages stakeholders in an open exchange of ideas, distilling each project to its essentials. In this way hidden potentials are often discovered, offering meaningful and relevant influences in project evolution, contextualization, and sustainability. nkA's synthesis of disciplines enables it to expand architectural practice beyond traditional boundaries, bringing clients into a collaborative and holistic process of design and building.

nkA is gaining recognition for a conscientious and detailed approach to their work. Viewing this as an affirmation of their commitment, the designers remain conscious that the measure of a project's success is not the professional accolades it receives; the architects' responsiveness to the individuality of the client and the project's parameters, context and environment, are the ultimate priorities of any project.

Nadège Patisserie
Toronto, ON

A restrained approach to design informs Nadège Patisserie, yielding a refined interior that is at once respectful and imaginative. This duality reinforces the dynamic of the Patisserie, juxtaposing the intimacy of the pastry display with the intensity of the open kitchen and surrounding social nodes.

The long, narrow proportions of the Patisserie are reinforced by a floating ceiling running the length of the interior, drawing patrons in from Queen Street West to the depths of the kitchen. This reading is reinforced by the clean lines of the white bar counter and seating, floating wall, and shelves, which stand in contrast to the grey, cavernous treatment of the interior's shell.

At the heart of these elements the extended, twenty-foot-long, gallery-like display of pastries engages patrons in an intimate "slow read" procession amidst the sights, smells, and sounds from the open kitchen, neighbouring park, street activity, and socializing patrons. This multi-sensory experience is created with minimal architectural means and by a transparency of process that allows the ambient sounds, aromas and energy to contrast with the pristine pastry display.

The seamless, neutral finishes and clean detailing of the Patisserie are a precise response to the owner's needs, and by keeping the focus on the centrepiece, the pastries, contribute to a rapidly growing business with a strong individual and corporate clientèle. An iconic Queen Street West landmark is re-established in a new light, and the site is transformed by an atmosphere of open friendliness where patrons are in the kitchen and the chef is amongst the people.

1

1   Concept diagrams and floor plan
2   Clean lines of floating shelves and ceiling contrast with grey shell
3   Seamless, neutral finishes maintain focus on product and brand
4   Twenty-foot-long gallery-like display of pastries engages patrons

3

4

Olivier Bourgeois Architecte

Quebec City, Québec

Olivier Bourgeois received his master's degree in architecture in 2006 from Laval University in Quebec City. He received the OAQ's Award of Excellence for his master's project, an arts complex in the Îles de la Madeleine (Magdelan Islands). He then worked with the architect Todd Saunders in Norway, where he learned about the power of landscape.

Bourgeois started his own practice in 2009. He teaches part time at Laval University and is regularly invited to sit on juries, participate in academic reviews, and give lectures. Bourgeois has been inspired in his young practice by the poetry of the landscape and also by the fundamental rules of maritime construction.

Bourgeois has been published in Canada and abroad in *Canadian Architect, Formes, ARQ, Wallpaper Magazine, Monsa Publications*, and on *Archdaily, Egodesign* and other architectural websites. He was invited to be part of the 2011 Architects Directory of Wallpaper Magazine.

<< D'ici la vue est libre

Trop de bleu
Magdalen Islands, QC

Trop de bleu is a temporary pavilion created in the Îles-de-la-Madeleine, an archipelago of small islands covered in dunes and colourful houses, surrounded by the blue water of the Gulf of St. Lawrence. The project was realized through a collaborative design process with Annie Landry, a local artist, photographer Serge Boudreau, and the architect. Five all-blue structures were installed along a crowded bikeway facing the sea and the infinite horizon. The structures were made of recycled wood studs covered with fibreglass sheets, using fishing-boat construction techniques learned from local experts.

Horizontality and constraint were the main sources of inspiration; the structures were designed with angles that evoke the erosion of the fragile landscape. The project appears like a breaking wave in an autumn storm, flowing over the site and lying naturally on this naked dusty landscape. Pedestrians were drawn to the new forms and their colour, pausing to look at the three large pictures and read the text printed on the structures, stimulating reflection and a sense of spiritual escape in the observer.

The main challenge was to create a contemporary project that respected both the site and the local user of the place. The power of *Trop de bleu* lies in its simplicity and its respectful dialogue with the natural and cultural landscape. Inspired by local tradition and fishermen's crafts, the artists merged tradition and modernity.

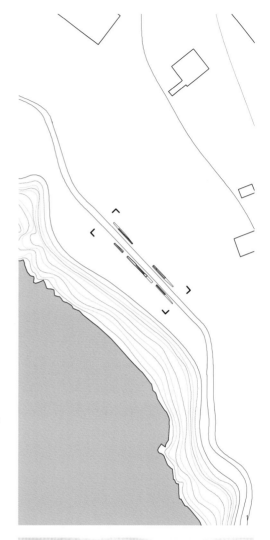

1 Site plan
2 Erosion of the landscape
3 Conceptual rendering
4 Maritime landscape
5 Poetry and photography along the bikeway
6 Blue wave over the landscape
7 Children playing on the structure

Olivier Bourgeois Architecte

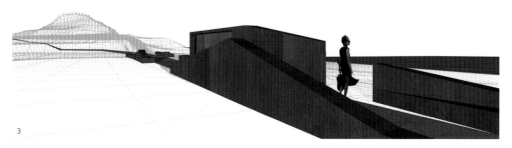

3

4

5

6

7

Omas
Toronto, Ontario

Brian O'Brian and Carl Muehleisen started
O'Brian Muehleisen Architecture Studio
(omas) in 2006 in New York City. The current
practice continues the collaboration as Brian
works from the Toronto studio of omas44 while
Carl operates from omas41 in New York.

Omas is interested in the expression of place,
which may be defined as a reaction to the specific
characteristics of site, context, client, and program.
Each project is pursued with a focus on its inherent
uniqueness, and with the intention of revealing
the sublime, in both built and un-built work.

With the partners' combined experience in design,
construction, and skilled trades, their work seeks to
foster an appreciation of craft, and to focus on the
means, methods and fabrication of form and space.

Urban Carriage House
New York, NY

During the design phase for the relatively modest, partial renovation of this 1903 carriage house on New York's Upper East Side, a portion of wall was removed, revealing the original brick, tile, and slate of the partition that had separated the horse barn and stalls from the enclosed carriage room. This discovery led to the full renovation of the first floor.

Materials that complemented the turn-of-the-century structure were used to reinvent the existing spaces with a language speaking to the current time and to the family's lifestyle. Inspired by the fact that the owners were avid wine collectors, white oak staves reclaimed from dismantled sherry casks were used to create the doors separating the two primary spaces on the floor. Blackened steel is employed in the entry doors, the suspended stair, and frame for the oak doors, recalling the building's history while maintaining a crispness of language reflective of current fabrication techniques. The existing opening in the rear wall was expanded and framed with steel and glass to allow more daylight into the family's everyday space. The existing wood floors were sanded, rubbed with white lye and finished with a matte sealer. In the kitchen and family room, new radiant-heated concrete floors were poured and polished. The walls are a rough white plaster, while the ceilings are a smooth and reflective Venetian plaster.

The upper floors carry through this aesthetic but with a softer approach. Bathrooms are tiled in white Statuario marble while the bedrooms are treated with muted tones. The top floor holds a glass box gym at its centre, allowing daylight to filter down from the skylight and traverse the floor, diffusing natural light within the upper landing gallery and library foyer.

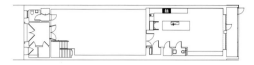
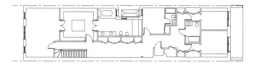
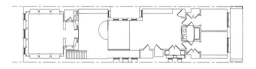

1

2

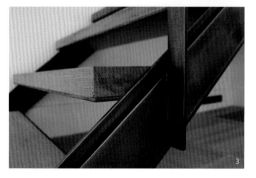

3

1   Floor plans
2   Front door peep slot detail
3   Stair detail
4   Dining room and gallery
5   View from kitchen through gallery to front door
6   Kitchen door detail: steel, glass, salvaged sherry cask oak

PARTISANS

Toronto, Ontario

PARTISANS is a Toronto-based research and design practice founded in 2010 by Alexander Josephson and Pooya Baktash. To survive in hard times, as unlicensed graduates at the nadir of the financial meltdown, they had to find new ways of working; PARTISANS had to become dissidents. The choice was clear: rot, or find a way to practice ambitious architecture at good value.

PARTISANS eliminated all middlemen from their projects. They became architects, construction managers, fabricators, and installers. Fortunately, they made a remarkable discovery—Toronto, it turns out, is a land of opportunity in a sea of economic turmoil. The Golden Horseshoe has an abundance of fabrication firms that previously served the automotive industry, knowledgeable in sophisticated technologies and large-scale manufacturing processes. This was the jackpot, a culture of accuracy, efficiency, delicacy, and material experimentation starving for exploitation. The practice was offered asylum. Partisans joined with this industry to marry cultural, material, and spatial forms of experimentation

Dedicated to ambitious architecture at all times, PARTISANS is working on scaleable architectures, from visualizations of statistical data mapped onto geographical space to experimental residential and commercial projects.

St Clair Eye Clinic
Toronto, ON

St Clair Eye Clinic is a state-of-the-art eye care facility located in the Oakwood and St. Clair neighbourhood in Toronto. The client, an ambitious young optometrist, wanted to be a catalyst for change in the area. He wanted an eyewear dispensary and clinic that felt like a living room and art gallery for local artists. He said he didn't need a spaceship, but PARTISANS begged to differ. A spaceship was exactly what his profession demanded. As the working relationship evolved, things began to change; the client's vision evolved and his vocabulary changed. It was as if there was a game of teaching between the client and the architects.

The clinic was imagined as an instrument of perception uniquely suited to the practice of a specialized profession: optometry. The space would be decidedly spaceship-like. The design called for a careful application of forced perspectival walls and shelving comprising an entire fifty-foot length of wall. These elements combined to produce a space that seemed much greater than the cramped envelope could possibly allow. The clinic included a dense program of offices, retail space, and diagnostics areas. The shelving was sculpted using advanced fabrications techniques (CNC) and the most unlikely and affordable of materials: expanded foam. Instead of using fine wood materials, PARTISANS took advantage of the unique forging and fabrication plants around the Toronto area that use recycled foam. The reason for using foam was twofold: first, it allowed for massive-scale objects at an affordable cost, and second, the objects could be manipulated by hand in the architects' own rented studios. Effectively, the illusion is twofold; the space appears larger and, with the cost of construction cleverly controlled, looks more expensive than it actually is.

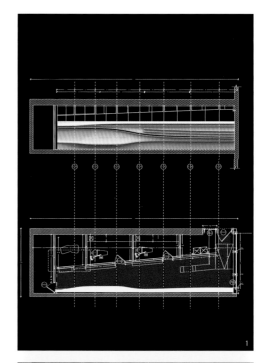

1   Plan and section
2   Exterior view
3   Interior view
4   Interior view

Temporary Mosque, Queen's Park

Toronto, ON

This temporary installation at Queen's Park was the culmination of a series of research projects on Islam at various scales: the histories and word, the prayer mat, and the mosque. The installation consisted of seventy-two high-impact polystyrene thermoforms oriented to within one-half of one degree of accuracy toward Mecca, Saudi Arabia. The installation was visited by hundreds of people and used by a number of practising and non-practising Muslims.

A mat supports the body. The function may be specific or general. The prayer mat developed here is designed for specific bodily positioning and has a utilitarian aspect in that it supports the needs of individual worshippers during Salaat, or prayers. A symbiotic relationship integrates the open concept of the work and its function as an expanded form of architecture or landscape in varying scales. The philosophical implications and physical parameters fuse religion and design, while making political comment through accretion.

The thermoforms work as tiles for use in parks and religious spaces. The fields of mats can also be imagined in vertical orientations, forming walls or a ceiling. There is also a metaphysical dimension to orientation, in that worship occurs with the human body oriented toward Mecca. This is critical to the communal and global aspects of Islam, associated with a non-biased interpretation of its histories, scriptures, and laws.

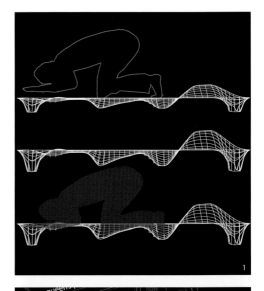

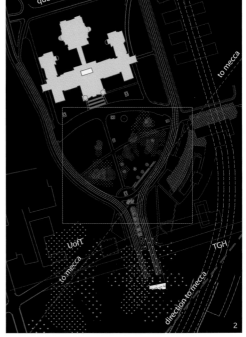

1   Diagram
2   Ghebleh
3   Panorama
4   Prayer

Public Architecture + Communication Inc.

Vancouver, British Columbia

Working collaboratively in cross-disciplinary teams, Public is combining architecture, technology, and information to create seamless buildings, environments, and stories.

The practice was founded in 2008 to explore the intersection of architecture and new forms of media, which are continually changing the way we design and experience space. Through collaboration between architects, environmental designers, and communication designers, the partners aim to provide a holistic, integrated approach that responds to the broad reach of their clients' needs—from buildings and signage to branding, identity, and other forms of graphic communication.

As a research agenda, the work focuses on the possibilities of "multivalent" public space through design inquiries that leverage digital technologies, emerging materials, and new construction techniques. These projects require close collaboration not only among design team members in the studio, but also with the consultants, fabricators, and building professionals tasked with execution. It is Public's conviction that good design is born of teamwork, rather than from the genius of a single author.

XTHUM

Surrey, BC

Xthum is a Hul'qumi'num word meaning "basket and drum."

A group acting on behalf of Kwantlen Polytechnic University and the Kwantlen, Semiahmoo, Tsawwassen, and Katzie Nations approached Public to design a multipurpose space within an existing classroom building for celebrating, feasting, storytelling, counseling, advising, studying, and relaxing.

The process began with a search for solutions to the project's biggest constraint — the program was too big for the 25-by-30-foot space provided. The design team settled on a strategy that anchors flexible zones of occupation around a fixed kitchen and fireplace element. Defining these zones is a ceiling/wall-scape that obscures references to the original former classroom: ceiling datums, corners, and existing windows are draped and concealed.

Given the client group's desire for a large, multifunctional centre, the interventions to the space reach up and out, establishing connections to the sky and adjacent forest. A roof monitor skylight draws natural light down into the centre of the space, while a vestibule addition becomes an east-facing entry that frames new First Nations artwork located near a stand of second-growth trees.

Contemporary construction and fabrication methodologies resonate with students whose nomadic cultural roots are a comfortable match with a nonstop contemporary lifestyle: studying at all hours, eating when convenient rather than at traditional meal times, these students are a technology-enabled group (an internet search for "First Nations blog," for example, yields more than 3 million results). The project is an exploration of digital design and output media, and also a lively dialogue between First Nations culture and the formal language of contemporary architecture.

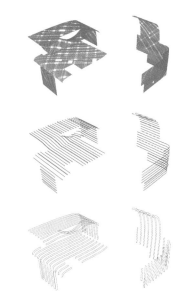

1

1   Structural hierarchy
2   Exploded axonometric
3   Fireplace and skylight
4   Ceiling detail
5   Overall view of room

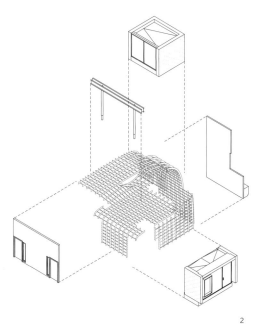

2

Public Architecture + Communication Inc.

Arts Pavilion and Identity

Vancouver, BC

Together with Phillips Farevaag Smallenberg, Public is merging landscape design, architecture, site furnishings, public art, identity, and signage to create a home for the arts on the UBC Point Grey campus.

The approach is to anchor the site around a pavilion to be used for festivals and public performances. The pavilion, set lightly within a reinstated reflecting pool, employs a six-inch-deep continuous folded concrete surface to achieve a fifty-foot span. A ribbon of new seating defines the east edge of the courtyard, providing places for learning outside the classroom. Two types of seating—the "slouch" and the "perch"—offer students different opportunities for relaxing, studying, and conversing.

Working with over twenty-five different departments and schools, Public also created a unified visual expression of the arts in the reflecting pool by means of an 800-word compilation of quotations from artists and writers in eleven different languages. This forms the foundation of the pavilion's new visual identity, which now incorporates Public's designs for building signage, presentation materials, T-shirts, and other signature items.

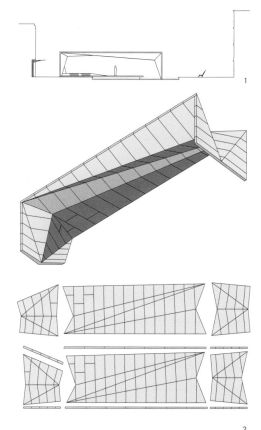

1

2

3

1   South elevation drawing of pavilion
2   Formwork studies of folded concrete plane
3   Covered bench detail
4   View from north-west
5   View from north
6   Slouch and perch bench

Rural / Urban / Fantasy / Project

Vancouver, British Columbia

Rural / Urban / Fantasy / Project is a
multidisciplinary design agency founded in 2008
and based in Vancouver. The partners, Sean
Pearson and Alyssa Schwann, seek to translate
ideas into immersive experiences, informed
by a rigorous aesthetic but always open to
crossing creative borders. The partners bring
different strengths to the work—Schwann is a
landscape architect and educator while Pearson
is an architect and branding specialist—yet
their finished work is a true collaboration,
in both the larger vision and the details.

Rather than starting with an idea of form, RUF
focuses on the experiential aspect of the space they
will create. Leaving behind any preconceived ideas
of a project, they allow the design to come out of
the narrative they weave with a client—whether it is
a landscape or a building or a branding concept.

The partners have wide-ranging international
experience, with projects completed in Europe,
Africa, and North America, yet their work is always
grounded in a certain Canadian sensibility, marked
by high design standards and originality. RUF is
committed to an *in situ* approach that respects the
local even as it references the global. Whether it
is the design of a private house that reinvigorates
the tradition of West Coast modernism, or the
design of a Soweto football training centre that
contributes to a new architectural language in
South Africa, RUF brings imagination and integrity
to each design challenge.

Gulf Islands Residence
Gulf Islands, BC

The design of this private residence responds to the clients' desire for a "modern log cabin" on a precious piece of oceanfront property. They were torn between two ideals: on the one hand the rustic Canadian log cabin and on the other the modernist glass house. Through the use of expressive structure, expanses of glass, and a minimal material palette, the project took this challenge as its fundamental concept, striving to reconcile the rustic with the modern in form, materiality, and organization.

A conscious decision was made to root the design of the house in the regional, west coast vernacular pioneered by architects such as Ron Thom and Arthur Erickson, beginning in the 1950s. The style is characterized by post-and-beam construction with exposed timber structural members, extensive glazing, open floor plans, interior-exterior links, wood finishes, flat roofs, orientation to views and a delicate balance with the natural setting. These elements were carefully integrated to define a new and innovative vision of regional architecture.

The house has been designed in the form of a bridge, creating a minimal footprint and achieving a high level of environmental performance on the site, while allowing native grasses and flora to grow underneath. Working with the topography, the house is defined in two parts—a solid stone base anchored to the land, referencing the existing rock outcrops on the site, and a light timber "bridge" resting on the stone. The strong horizontals of the heavy timber structure reference the horizon, and transparency on the ocean side opens the full house to stunning panoramic views of the sea.

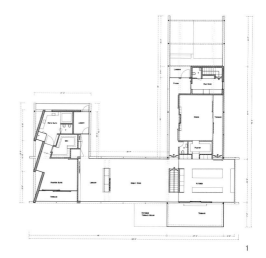

1

2

3

1   Upper level plan
2   View towards house
3   Boathouse
4   Entry and courtyard
5   Kitchen terrace and panoramic views
6   Kitchen
7   Master bedroom

Rural / Urban / Fantasy / Project

Camo Density: or how I learned to love living in a hedge

Vancouver, BC

With a rental vacancy rate under one percent and high levels of immigration, Vancouver is facing a housing crisis. Demand for central living accommodation is increasing, and because there are very few urban lots available for development, attention should be directed at spaces within the city's single-unit neighbourhoods of detached houses. This proposal suggests an alternative to urban densification, or suburban sprawl, while maintaining the "urban green ways" of Vancouver's existing neighbourhoods.

The city owns a large amount of land in the form of boulevards along a number of Vancouver's wider streets, and these spaces could potentially be used without adverse impact on the character of the neighbourhoods. The proposed solution is to create pre-manufactured units that could be stacked, linked linearly, and connected to the existing underground services running under the streets and boulevards. In contrast to the creation of new suburban subdivisions, which would mean the destruction of more of the natural landscape in Greater Vancouver's surrounding mountains or further encroachment on the precious farmland in the Delta, this solution makes use of existing urban space with no need for investment in new services and streets.

Inspired by Vancouver's green streets, and especially its hedges, this design proposes a series of 16-by-25-foot pre-manufactured hedge units, with construction techniques and material usage kept extremely simple to expedite production and minimize waste. Each unit would be constructed of a steel frame, with concrete-slab-on-steel-deck for the roof, and floor slabs and a double-glazed frameless curtain wall. An integrated planting tray around the perimeter with hydroponically grown hedges creates an outer skin. A roof pond, acting as a skylight and also a collector of rainwater and grey water, would irrigate the hedges. The pond would also be used to supply the thermal in-floor radiant heating system.

1

2

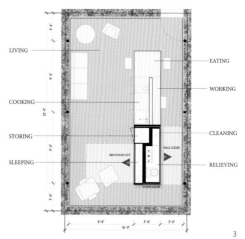

LIVING
COOKING
STORING
SLEEPING

EATING
WORKING
CLEANING
RELIEVING

3

1   Topiary + Modernist prefabricated construction + Vancouver boulevard
2   Possible variations of hedge arrangement
3   Floor plan
4   View down boulevard with hedge-houses
5   Interior view

Rural / Urban / Fantasy / Project

Football Training Centre

Soweto, South Africa

Situated in the heart of Soweto, the Football Training Centre is the focus and de facto headquarters for football in all of South Africa; 1,200 teams and 20,000 footballers play here each year. The redesign created by RUF for Nike South Africa took less than six months to complete and transformed the facility into a state-of-the-art training centre, the first of its kind not only in Africa but in the entire world. The complex has two full-sized new artificial pitches, two junior turf pitches, new lighting, a clubhouse and players' lounge, an education section for the Grass Roots Soccer & Life Skillz program, a training gym, physiotherapy and first aid offices, a new space for product trials and catering, an administrative centre, viewing deck, and change rooms. The clubhouse and players' lounge provides a place for coaches and players to focus on the tactical and strategic aspects of the game.

The programs of the facility are linked, visually and physically, by a clear but intricately woven relationship of spaces achieved through "cuts" in the solid mass of the rectangular structure. The design was created for and around the players, supporting the various aspects of their day. Everything possible has been done to allow the facility to flow and remain open, while at the same time managing the real need for a secure and safe place to play football.

1   The fields
2   Entrance
3   North façade and fields
4   North façade at night

Rural / Urban / Fantasy / Project

97

studio junction inc.
Toronto, Ontario

Established in 2004 by Peter Tan and
Christine Ho Ping Kong, studio junction draws on
the experience and knowledge that comes with their
combined degrees in architecture and fine arts. Since
forming their small studio and custom woodworking
shop they have undertaken architectural, design,
and construction projects involving diverse spaces
and objects of various scales. Their portfolio includes
free-standing and built-in furniture, temporary
exhibitions and installations, pre-fabricated
structures, interiors, and renovated and new houses.
The studio's process is collaborative and site-driven;
the focus is on creating small intimate spaces, open
to natural light and connected to the outdoors.

studio junction inc. has been widely recognized for
the Courtyard House, which reflects their interest
in urbanism, the poetics of light and space, and
the detailing and craft of woodworking. Although
they are a young firm, their work has received many
awards and has been reviewed in local, national, and
international publications. They were named one
of the "10 to Watch" in 2009 by the *Toronto Star*.

Current projects include a photography studio,
a barrier-free house, an urban shop/house,
and infill housing in Kensington Market.

Courtyard House
Toronto, ON

The Courtyard House was inspired by an ancient form of architecture and a desire to experiment with a new form of urban thinking—infill housing as an alternative North American urban typology. Studio junction's challenge was to convert a contractor's warehouse in a mixed-use industrial neighbourhood into an affordable home and studio for a family of four, and to create a successful adaptation in a mid-block or laneway space, where there is no typical front or back. The design was generated by an emphasis on the views and activities of traditional interior courtyards, where all the windows look inwards.

While the exterior façade is blank and monolithic, the interior is transparent. An open ground-floor plan and two sets of sliding doors allow for long views through the house, towards the varied activities in the courtyard. Conceived as a series of horizontal strata, the ground floor includes a home office, dining room, kitchen, and living room, with a studio across the courtyard. The more private second floor includes bedrooms and an elongated bathroom/laundry room which opens onto an upper terrace. Natural light is captured by the courtyard, skylights, and clerestory windows. The walk-through offers an experience that alternates between open and covered areas, light and shade, indoors and outdoors, and a poetic "space in between."

The limited material palette of masonry and wood is used to express the playful push and pull between exterior and interior. Openings were made in the monolithic exterior block wall and at these strategic cuts, the wood cladding highlights the volume and suggests a warm residential habitation hidden within. The courtyard, open to the sky, acts as an oasis and intimate room in a dense urban environment. In the summer it is an enclosed play area for the children and an active living space to cook, eat, and linger outdoors. In the fall, winter, and spring the courtyard and the Japanese maple are the link to the changing seasons, as they bring the outdoors in and mark the passage of time.

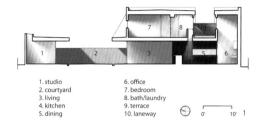

1. studio
2. courtyard
3. living
4. kitchen
5. dining
6. office
7. bedroom
8. bath/laundry
9. terrace
10. laneway

0'   10'   1

1   Section
2   Upper terrace
3   Hallway with translucent screen wall
4   View of courtyard, looking towards studio
5   Child's bed/room with translucent sliding doors

studio junction inc.

T B A

Montréal, Québec

T B A is a small but growing multidisciplinary studio
focusing on architecture and design. The award-
winning practice, established by Tom Balaban in
2009, is currently involved in residential, commercial,
and small-scale institutional projects that focus on
making cultural contributions, while also providing
meaningful social and physical experiences.

T B A does not give preference to any single rhetoric,
tool, or method. Committed to the principle that
good architecture does not emerge from marking
off items on a checklist of bells and whistles, the
studio approaches architecture as a balanced system
of interrelated hard and soft issues. Each project is
highly responsive to its time and context. Moreover,
each project is a direct result of its own specific
evolution and process, and is achieved by the means
and methods best suited to the desired outcome.

The studio is also engaged in parallel research
and speculative work and its designers are active
participants in the academic environment.
They seek out every opportunity to challenge
standard conditions, expand current conventions,
and create better environments.

Amphitheatre Trois-Rivières

Trois-Rivières, QC

The competition called for a new amphitheatre, strategically situated on a site previously occupied by Trois-Rivières' last pulp-and-paper mill, at the intersection of the St. Lawrence and St-Maurice rivers, at the edge of the city's historic centre. The project brief was to create a 10,000-seat, partially covered amphitheatre, a bandshell, and a park complex to house a wide range of music series and annual performing arts events.

Proposing a dialogue between a contemporary intervention and a site laden with history, the architects lifted the existing landscape to make room for the amphitheatre. The elevated terrain became an abstract marquee, rising high enough to house administrative offices and dressing rooms, as well as technical operations or equipment. Accessible via a retractable stair, the rooftop terrain also provides a spectacular view over the intersection of the two rivers. Where there was once an abrupt drop to the river, the new topography now cascades below the roof's chromed underside, flowing down from the new public plaza through the amphitheatre to the river boardwalk below. During the winter, the stage is transformed into a reception hall and small theatre, integrating the project year-round into the cultural landscape of Trois-Rivières.

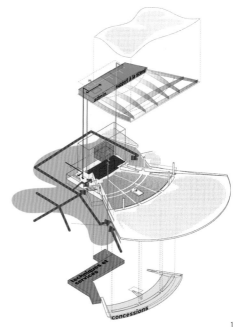

1

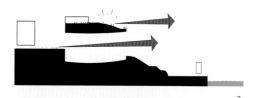

2

3

1   Exploded axonometric
2   Concept diagram
3   Concept image
4   View from main plaza
5   View from seating area
6   Massing model

Lalonde-Gadoury Residence

Montréal, QC

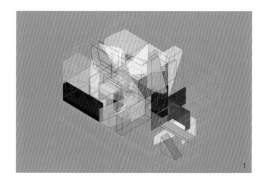

This project, undertaken for a small family, consisted of a complete interior renovation of a semi-detached duplex on the edge of Outremont. The clients were looking to shrink an existing rental unit and, in turn, expand their own home. Using a series of three-dimensional light studies, T B A established a new spatial organization that maximized the available natural light in each area, with minor interventions on the envelope. Axonometric models, with blocks representing the cumulative light at a specific time of day throughout the year, were used as light studies to determine where to place the rooms, walls, and openings on each floor, keeping in mind what time of day each space was most likely to be occupied. All three models were used simultaneously to establish the structure of the space and the placement of room divisions.

Interconnecting spaces and strategic enlargements of a few openings in the side and rear allowed both views and light to penetrate the house and the apartment, without sacrificing privacy. On the ground floor, the structure was reconfigured and replaced with furniture elements that create an open reading of the plan and a continuous connection to the garden. The spatial strategies now allow the daily function of the house to follow in step with the movement of the sun throughout the day. Moreover, unexpected double-height spaces and opportune views to the exterior create a varied set of experiences inside the relatively boxy volume of the original structure.

1   Axonometric process drawing
2   Perforated ceiling at ground floor
3   Living room and garden
4   First floor corridor
5   Main stair
6   Dining room

WE-DESIGNS.ORG, LLC

Vancouver, British Columbia

Conceived in 2003 and officially launched as
a collective in 2008, WE-DESIGNS.ORG is an
international multidisciplinary creative group with
bases in Vancouver, New York, Hong Kong and
Vienna. The practice's design projects are conceived
and implemented by a team of creative individuals
working collaboratively, seeking to maintain the
highest standards of architecture and design. Their
goal is to establish detail-oriented quality within
multiple design functions, including material
research, alternative fabrication methods, sound
design, interactive installation, architectural/urban
planning, and research-based design strategies.

The WE-DESIGNS.ORG team members are an
international base of young designers bringing
fresh ideas from their distinctive backgrounds
and different fields. Experimental innovations and
theoretical approaches are integrated into each
project after all ideas and points of view have been
considered.

Cross-Fabricated Scales

Singapore/Hong Kong, HK

Cross-Fabricated Scales is an investigative prototype demonstrating a crossover between architecture and art; an experiment utilizing geometry and materials research that focuses on the developmental nature of experimentation, and makes use of details resulting from the scalability of a singular, yet repeated, patterning unit.

The emphasis of this piece is on the seamless transition between scales of a composite geometry based on an evolution of typologies; it also offers an exploration of the physical properties intrinsic to the technique of digital and analog design experimentations. In fostering the synthesis of repetition and variation within a scalable logic, *Cross-Fabricated Scales* focuses its design experimentation on the challenge of producing a continuous surface condition in a composite unit that has the ability to scale up through the minimal connection of parts.

The form-finding investigation and evaluation included active laboratory testing of physical models, in conjunction with computer simulation and optimization processes through a CNC (3D) milled prototype of the individual modules, which could then be attached to a framing system. In addition, the fragility of the forms and differentiated materials was assessed through experimentation during the design development and research process.

The final [whole] wall is constructed of modular self-supporting aggregates that seamlessly unite through a minimal connection of parts, creating a gradient of tessellation across scales. The complete unit has the potential to scale *ad infinitum*, yet the perception of its parts is diffused through its design such that it expresses a maximum variation with a minimum number of parts, while also allowing for ease of transport and construction. In order to fully express the effect of the scalar transition, the repeated units are best viewed as a formalized wall or partition system, which can either divide or enclose space.

1   Exploded module
2   Physical HI-MACS Prototype B
3   Diagrammatic breakdown of modulars
4   Grasshopper digital tooling line drawing
5   Interior context render

1

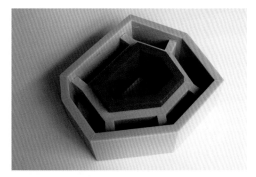

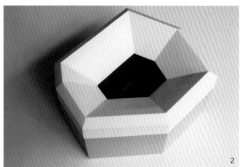

2

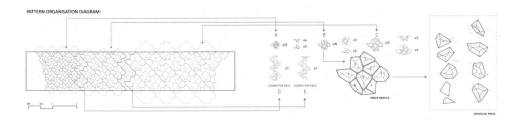

PATTERN ORGANISATION DIAGRAM:

3

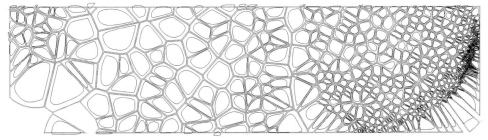

4

5

Up : Urban Tower Transformation

Surrey, BC

UP is an investigation into the urban tower building type. Organized around the geometry of the hexagon, two-dimensional studies were made and translated to a three-dimensional rationale, and then developed into an accentuated folded landscape.

The folding landscapes of the public space and residential tower offer a bold and playful extension of the ground plan, integrating a multi-storey tower with an urban park high in the sky. This folding landscape is achieved by an articulated system that, overcoming traditional tectonic hierarchies, provides structural economy and thereby increases useable floor area.

The folding landscape of public space offers a lively venue for social activity and interaction, while bringing greenery close to the user at every level. The folds of the multi-level open public space allow for various public and community programs, while the structural geometries develop continuities of openness and privacy that humanize the scale of the project. The intertwining of public space and the tower, as the design folds into itself and through the site, integrates the natural surroundings into the urban spectrum. Additionally, the multi-faceted façade of the tower offers beautiful views for all of the residences.

Within the folding residential layout is an integrated piping system that collects, processes, and recycles rainwater and grey water from the building for reuse, specifically for heating and irrigation purposes; uses that do not require potable water. This sustainable self-generating system allows the building to maintain itself without a secondary water supply. The use of bio-glass as a material and the forms of the window curvature combine to maximize the thermal absorption of sunlight and balance the windows' performance between reflectivity and materiality, in effect neutralizing the sun's heat in summer and yet allowing its warmth into the building in winter.

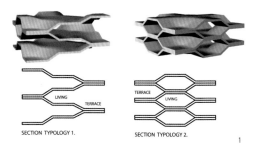

SECTION TYPOLOGY 1.

SECTION TYPOLOGY 2.

1

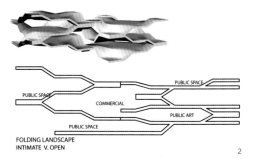

FOLDING LANDSCAPE
INTIMATE V. OPEN

2

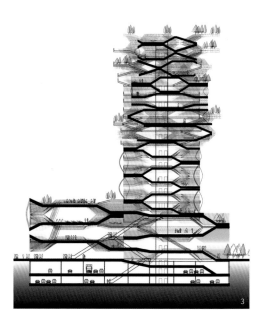

3

1 Section typology
2 Diagrammatic folding landscape
3 Diagrammatic section
4 Northeast day render
5 Southwest close-up render

Project Credits

5468796 Architecture Inc.

266 McDermot Avenue
Winnipeg, Manitoba R3B 0S8
T 204 480 8421
www.5468796.ca
info@5468796.ca

OMS Stage
Design team: Sharon Ackerman, Mandy
Aldcorn, Ken Borton, Michelle Heath, Aynslee
Hurdal, Johanna Hurme, Cristina Ionescu, Grant
Labossiere, Colin Neufeld, Zach Pauls, Sasa
Radulovic, Shannon Wiebe
Location: Winnipeg, Manitoba
Completion: 2010
Project Manager: Mark Penner (Greenseed
Development Corporation)
Structural: Lavergne Draward & Associates
Electrical: MCW - Age
Lighting: Ambiances Lighting + Visual Design
Photography: 5468796 Architecture Inc.

Centre Village
Design Team: Sharon Ackerman, Mandy
Aldcorn, Ken Borton, Michelle Heath, Aynslee
Hurdal, Johanna Hurme, Cristina Ionescu, Grant
Labossiere, Colin Neufeld, Zach Pauls, Sasa
Radulovic, Shannon Wiebe; with Cohlmeyer
Architecture: Stephen Cohlmeyer, Stephanie
Aastrom, Dirk Blouw, Czesia Bulowska, Randolph
Dico, Daniel Enns, Heinrich Hendrix, David
Weber
Location: Winnipeg, Manitoba
Completion: 2010
Construction: Capstone Construction
Structural: Lavergne Draward & Associates
Landscape Design: Cynthia Cohlmeyer
Photographs: 5468796 Architecture Inc.

Acre Architects

5 Westview Drive
Saint John, New Brunswick E2K 2G6
T 506 658 9679
www.theacre.ca
info@theacre.ca

In transit
Design Team: Stephen Kopp, Monica Adair
Location: Saint John, New Brunswick
Completion: 2009
Construction: Sojourn Enterprises
Photography: Mark Hemmings

Alec Brown Architect

1672 Barrington Street
Halifax, Nova Scotia B3J 2A2
T 902 802 0481
www.alecbrownarchitect.ca
contact@alecbrownarchitect.ca

Cross Passage House
Design Team: Alec Brown
Location: Lunenburg, Nova Scotia
Completion: 2009
Construction: D. Risser Construction Ltd.
Structural: Andrea Doncaster, P.Eng.
Photography: Alec Brown Architect, Stephan
Hederich

Atelier Kastelic Buffey Inc.

203- 176 John Street
Toronto, Ontario M5T 1X5
T 416 204 1331
www.akb.ca
info@akb.ca

Maison Glissade
Design Team: Kelly Buffey, Robert Kastelic,
Artur Kobylanski, Terry Sin, Caileigh MacKeller,
Jonathan Lim, Sabrina Richard
Location: Collingwood, Ontario
Completion: 2010
Construction: Wilson Project Management
Photography: Shai Gil

Chevalier Morales Architectes

5455 avenue de Gaspé, suite 1000
Montréal, Québec H2T 3B3
T 514 273 9277
www.chevaliermorales.com

Spa at Nuns' Island
Design Team: Sergio Morales, Stephan Chevalier,
Karine Dieujuste, Christine Giguère, Samantha
Hayes, Neil Melendez
Location: Montréal, Québec
Completion: 2009
Construction: Pomerleau
Engineering: Les Consultants Gemec, Génivar
Consultants: Eau de gamme (exterior baths)
Photography: Marc Cramer (2,3,4,6) / Alexandre
Massé (title image, 5)

Great Lake Studio

122 Harrison Street
Toronto, Ontario M6J 2A3
T 416 828 6982
www.greatlakestudio.ca
rick@greatlakestudio.ca

Temagami Wilderness Camp
Design Team: Rick Galezowski
Location: Temagami, Ontario
Completion: 2010
Renderings: Rick Galezowski, Maggie Bennedsen

Idea Tank Design Collective

4- 2 Spadina Rd
Toronto, Ontario M5R 2S7
T 647 893 7982
www.ideatank.ca
a.choptiany@gmail.com

Camp at Cabot Beach
Design Team: Clayton Blackman, Andrew
Choptiany, Mark Erickson, Matthew Kennedy,
Sam Lock
Location: Malpeque, Prince Edward Island
Completion: 2009
Photography: Idea Tank Design Collective

Matthew Soules Architecture Inc.

2968 Mathers Crescent
West Vancouver, British Columbia V7V 2L3
T 604 568 1050
www.msaprojects.com
office@msaprojects.com

Victoria Public Urinal
Design Team: Matthew Soules, Mike Wartman
Location: Victoria, British Columbia
Completion: 2010
Construction: Aral Construction Ltd.
Photography: Matthew Soules Architecture

McMinn + Janzen Studio

409 Shaw Street
Toronto, Ontario M6J 2X4
T 416 530 0088
www.mjarch.ca
melana.janzen@gmail.com

CP Harbour House
Design Team: Melana Janzen, John McMinn
Location: Big Bay, Ontario
Completion: 2011
Construction: Ken Burrows and Son Contracting
Structural: Blackwell Bowick Partnership Ltd.
Photography: Terence Tourangeau

_naturehumaine [architecture+design]

305 rue de Bellechasse Est, Bureau 308
Montréal, Québec H2S 1W9
T 514 273 6316
www.naturehumaine.com
nh@naturehumaine.com

De La Congrégation Residence
Design Team: Stéphane Rasselet, Marc-André
Plasse, Amélie Melaven, Olivier Lajeunesse-
Travers
Location: Montréal, Québec
Completion: 2010
Construction: Sienna Construction
Photography: Marc-André Plasse

St-Hubert Residence
Design Team: Marc-André Plasse, Stéphane
Rasselet, Amélie Melaven, Olivier Lajeunesse-
Travers, Anne-Marie Nguyen
Location: Montréal, Québec
Completion: 2010
Construction: Constructions JJL
Photography: Marc-André Plasse

nkArchitect

G10 - 101 Duncan Mill Road
Toronto, Ontario M3B 1Z3
T 416 642 6199
www.nkarchitect.ca
nka@nkarchitect.ca

Nadège Patisserie
Design Team: Nelson Kwong, Neal Prabhu, Leroy
Shum, Eline Lu
Location: Toronto, Ontario
Completion: 2010
Construction: Morgan McHugh
Photography: Peter A. Sellar

Olivier Bourgeois Architecte

308- 7 St-Vallier est
Quebec City, Québec G1K 3N6
T 418 580 6548
www.bourgeoislechasseur.com
obourgeois@bourgeoislechasseur.com

Trop de bleu
Design Team: Olivier Bourgeois
Location: Îles-de-la-Madeleine, Québec
Completion: 2009
Carpenter: Gaston Bourgeois, Cyrice Boudreau
Fibreglass Specialist: Les Entreprises Leo Leblanc
& fils
Visual Artist: Annie Landry
Photography: Serge Boudreau, Olivier Bourgeois

Omas

3 Gilead Place
Toronto, Ontario M5A 3C8
T 416 900 6862
www.omasworks.com
architects@omasworks.com

Urban Carriage House
Design Team: Brian O'Brian, Carl Muehleisen
Location: New York, New York
Completion: 2008
Construction: SMI Construction Management,
Inc.
Lighting: Richard J Shaver Architectural Lighting
Photography: Kathryn Kalajian Photography

PARTISANS

1 Yorkville Avenue
Toronto, Ontario M4W 1L1
T 416 388 4803
www.partisanprojects.com
info@partisanprojects.com

St Clair Eye Clinic
Design Team: Alex Josephson, Pooya Baktash,
Shamir Panchal, Zak McPherson, Laila Salti
Location: Toronto, Ontario
Completion: 2010
Construction: Coia build
Fabrication: Tim Sheppard, Kal Mansur, Mike
Greenwood
Photography: Steve Tsai Photography

Temporary Mosque
Design Team: Alex Josephson, Pooya Baktash
Location: Toronto, Ontario
Completion: 2008
Fabrication: Canadian Plastics Group, Anselmi
Foundry
Photographs: Toronto Star Photography

Public Architecture + Communication Inc.

215– 309 W Cordova Street
Vancouver, British Columbia V6B 1E5
T 604 738 4323
www.publicdesign.ca
info@publicdesign.ca

XTHUM
Design Team: Chris Forrest, Susan Mavor, Matty
Scolozzi, Brian Wakelin, John Wall, David Zeibin
Location: Surrey, British Columbia
Completion: 2009
Construction: Parkwood Construction
Structural: Bush Bohlman and Partners
Woodworking: Pacific Woodworking
Furnishing: Inform Interiors
Photography: Nic Lehoux

Arts Pavilion and Identity
Design Team: Chris Forrest, Susan Mavor, Brian
Wakelin, John Wall
Location: Vancouver, British Columbia
Completion: 2011
Construction: Scott Construction
Landscape Architect: Phillips Farevaag
Smallenberg
Structural: Fast + Epp
Fountain Mechanical: Vincent Helton
Fabrication: 3D Services
Photography: Public Architecture +
Communication

Rural / Urban / Fantasy / Project

260 - 49 Dunlevy Avenue
Vancouver, British Columbia V6A 3A3
T 604 569 3282
www.rufproject.com
info@rufproject.com

Gulf Island's Residence
Design Team: Sean Pearson, Alyssa Schwann
Location: Gulf Islands, British Columbia
Completion: 2011
Construction: H. Hazenboom Construction Ltd.
Structural: Bengt Jansson, Parallel Structural
Engineers
Building Envelope Consultant: Richard Kadulski
Architect
Photography: Ivan Hunter

Camo Density
Design Team: Sean Pearson, Alyssa Schwann
Location: Vancouver, British Columbia
Completion: 2010
Renderings: Sean Pearson, Alyssa Schwann

Football Training Centre
Design Team: Sean Pearson, Nike Global Football
(Creative Director Andy Walker)
Location: Soweto, South Africa
Completion: 2010
Construction: Rainbow Construction
Project Management: SIP Project Managers Ltd.
Local Architect: Design Space Africa
Graphics: Grid Worldwide Branding & Design
Photography: Julian Abrams

studio junction inc.

2087 Davenport Road (rear)
Toronto, Ontario M6N 1C9
T 416 652 3906
www.studiojunction.ca
info@studiojunction.ca

Courtyard House
Design Team: Peter Tan, Christine Ho Ping Kong
Location: Toronto, Ontario
Completion: 2007
Construction: studio junction
Photography: Rob Fiocca

Project Credits

T B A

210-b Mozart Avenue West
Montréal, Québec H2S 1C4
T 514 583 5838
www.t--b--a.com
info@t--b--a.com

Amphitheater Trois-Rivières
Design Team: Tom Balaban, Andrew Chau,
Jennifer Thorogood
Location: Trois-Rivières, Québec
Completion: 2010
Renderings: Andrew Chau

Lalonde-Gadoury Residence
Design Team: Tom Balaban, Rami Abou-Khalil,
Matthew Balean, Justine Chibuk
Location: Montréal, Québec
Completion: 2008
Construction: ER Gestion Rénovation
Photography: TBA

WE-DESIGNS.ORG, LLC

53 West Hastings Street
Vancouver, British Columbia V6B 1G4
T 604 518 2809
www.we-designs.org
together@we-designs.org

Cross-Fabricated Scales
Design Team: Wendy W Fok, Sue Y Biolsi
Location: Singapore, Hong Kong
Completion: In-Progress
Technical Consultant: Daniela Kröhnert
Material Consultant: DuPont Corian Asia Pacific,
LG Hausys - HI-MACS
Prototype fabricator: Luxx Newhouse Group Pte
Renderings/drawings: Wendy W Fok (1,3,5), Sue
Y Biolsi (3), Daniela Kröhnert (4)

Up – Urban Tower Transformation
Design Team: Kadri Kerge, Wendy W Fok, Jenny
Chow, Sue Y Biolsi, Vasilis Raptis, Viktorie
Senešová
Location: Surrey, British Columbia
Completion: 2010
Renderings: Jenny Chow (3), Wendy W Fok (2,4),
Kadri Kerge (1-5)

Essay Authors

Will Jones is a British-born construction professional turned architectural journalist and author who now lives in Haliburton, Ontario. He has been writing for architecture and design magazines around the world for over 15 years. Publications featuring his work include *A10* and *Frame* in the Netherlands, Canada's *Elemente*, *DAMn* from Belgium, *Blueprint*, *Building* and the *RIBA Journal* in the UK and Australia's *Green Magazine*. He is the author of several books, including *New Transport Architecture*, *Modern Architecture in New York* and *Unbuilt Masterworks of the 21st Century*. His latest book, *Architects' Sketchbook*, has recently been published globally, with co-editions being sold in French, Italian and Japanese language.

Peter Sampson is a graduate of the School of Architecture at the University of Toronto and received a degree in Literature from McGill University. He writes for *Canadian Architect* and has taught at the Universities of Manitoba, Waterloo, and Toronto. Peter Sampson Architecture Studio Inc. is located in Winnipeg and consists of ten staff. Current commissions include urban design, municipal and educational facilities, recreation and wellness centres, projects fabricated from reclaimed sea containers, and net-zero energy housing. Peter is a founding a partner of the DPA+PSA+DIN Collective, the architect of Plug-In ICA and the University of Winnipeg's new Buhler Centre in downtown Winnipeg.

Twenty + Change Directors

Heather Dubbeldam is the Principal of Dubbeldam Design Architects, a multi-disciplinary architecture practice in Toronto. The firm has been recognized with many awards including the OAA 2008 Best Emerging Practice award, and has been published in local, national and international publications. Dubbeldam plays an active role in the design and architecture community: as Co-Director of Twenty + Change, promoting emerging architecture and design practices across Canada; as Co-Chair of the Toronto Society of Architects; and as a Director of the Design Industry Advisory Committee, a provincial not-for-profit, cross-disciplinary design think tank and research group. She was co-editor of the award-winning TSA *Toronto Architecture Guide Map* and co-editor, with Lola Sheppard, of the Twenty + Change 01 & 02 publications.

Lola Sheppard is Assistant Professor at the University of Waterloo, School of Architecture. She is a partner at Lateral Office, and a Director of InfraNet Lab. Lateral Office was the recipient of the 2011 Emerging Voices Award and the 2005 Young Architects Forum from the Architectural League of New York and was awarded the 2010 Prix de Rome from the Canada Council for the Arts. Sheppard recently co-authored *Coupling: Strategies for Infrastructural Opportunism* (Princeton Architectural Press, 2011) and she is co-editor of the upcoming *Bracket 2: Soft Systems* (Actar, 2011). She is also co-editor, with Heather Dubbeldam, of the Twenty + Change 01 & 02 publications. She is currently pursuing research and design work on architecture, infrastructure and urbanism in Canada's far North.

Twenty + Change 03 Sponsors

Twenty + Change would like to thank the following sponsors who generously helped make this exhibition and publication possible.

Lead Sponsor
DIALOG

Publication Sponsors
Canada Council for the Arts
Astley Gilbert Limited

Supporting Sponsors
Ciot
Forbo Flooring Systems

Exhibition Print Sponsor
Astley Gilbert Limited

Exhibition Sponsors
Blackwell Bowick Partnership Limited
Engineered Assemblies
Stone Tile International Inc.
Royal Architectural Institute of Canada

Donations-in-kind
Harbourfront Centre, Toronto